The Renewal of Catholic Higher Education

By
CHARLES E. FORD
and
EDGAR L. ROY, JR.

Report of a study of Catholic higher education conducted under the auspices of the College and University Department, National Catholic Educational Association, through a grant from the Ford Foundation's Fund for the Advancement of Education.

Additional copies of this publication may be obtained from the National Catholic Educational Association, 1785 Massachusetts Avenue, N.W., Washington, D.C. 20036.

Price: $3.50 prepaid.

NATIONAL CATHOLIC EDUCATIONAL ASSOCIATION
Washington, D.C.

1785 Massachusetts Avenue, N.W., Washington, D.C. 20036
Library of Congress Catalog Card No. 68-25998
Manufactured in the United States of America

NATIONAL CATHOLIC EDUCATIONAL ASSOCIATION COMMITTEE ON CATHOLIC HIGHER EDUCATION

CONTENTS

FOREWORD

In March 1964, Reverend Paul C. Reinert, S.J., President of Saint Louis University, told the College and University Department of the National Catholic Educational Association that there is a vital need for a carefully prepared, flexible blueprint for Catholic higher education. He encouraged the Department to undertake a basic study of Catholic colleges and universities upon which recommendations for the future might be based. In late spring of 1964, an Advisory Committee of the College and University Department of the NCEA was formed. Bishop James Shannon, then President of Saint Thomas College in St. Paul, Minn., was selected as chairman, with the responsibility of directing preparation of a report.

Funds for the study were granted by the Ford Foundation's Fund for the Advancement of Education. Dr. Charles E. Ford, former Assistant Professor of Education at Saint Louis University and now Vice President of Fontbonne College in St. Louis, was chosen as Director of Research. Dr. Edgar L. Roy, Jr., former Assistant to the President of Saint Louis University and now Vice President of the College of Our Lady of Mercy, Burlingame, Calif., was engaged as Research Associate. *The Renewal of Catholic Higher Education* is the final report prepared for the Advisory Committee by the research staff. With the unanimous endorsement of the Committee, it is here presented to those interested in an responsible for the current status and future development of Catholic higher education in the United States.

Catholic higher education is no longer a subject of concern only to those more or less directly involved in the operation of Catholic colleges and universities. Speculations about the status and future of Catholic higher education, articles dealing with trouble on

Catholic campuses, and features highlighting the delicate relationship between Catholic institutions of higher learning and the Catholic hierarchy are now appearing with considerable regularity in the popular press. Some of the publicity given Catholic institutions has been favorable; much has not. The accuracy of many articles has been questioned. Basically, however, the motivation underlying most of the articles in the popular press has been that of capitalizing on the contemporary interest of the American public both in higher education and in religion, more than of deliberately campaigning either to smear or to promote Catholic higher education as such. Consequently, much of the publicity deals with sensational material. This, unfortunately, suggests a critical condition of uncertainty and trouble within Catholic higher education. Some of those responsible for the future of Catholic higher education are of the opinion that this exposure is doing more harm than good. Others, while regretting the inaccuracies, see this popular pressure as a catalyst for initiating needed changes.

Opinions vary among Catholic educators not only about the advantages and disadvantages that current publicity is bringing to Catholic higher education but also about the very format of publicity that contributes most to Catholic higher education. Some authors seem to think that an enumeration of the weaknesses of Catholic institutions is more effective than a discussion of the strengths of Catholic higher education. Other writers are convinced that preaching the positive is better than breast-beating.

The motivation and the method of the present report must be seen in the light of the abundance of current publicity about Catholic higher education and the variety of approaches of such publicity.

The members of the Advisory Committee responsible for this report are all deeply involved in Catholic higher education and are openly dedicated to its stated goals and future good. Moreover, the Committee is of the opinion that these goals and this good in no way conflict with the commitment of each Catholic college and university to the goals and ultimate good of American higher education. In fact, the Committee takes the stand that Catholic higher education may be strengthened specifically through the correct understanding and improvement of Catholic higher education.

Some concern has been voiced by Catholic educators over the format of the Advisory Committee's preliminary *Working Paper.* This document, prepared by the Committee's research staff and privately distributed to Catholic institutions, dealt exclusively with contemporary weaknesses and problems in Catholic colleges and universities. The preface of the *Working Paper* specifically called attention to the fact that, although the problems and weaknesses enumerated do exist in Catholic institutions, not all of the problems exist on all the campuses and not all institutions experience either the weaknesses or the problems to the same degree. However, some Catholic administrators believed that the *Working Paper* could be misunderstood and thus could bring more harm than good to Catholic higher education. These administrators maintained that some colleges and universities had already overcome the problems enumerated in the *Working Paper,* or that the problems applied more aptly to small or weak institutions.

The Advisory Committee recognizes the risk involved in any instance of honest and open recognition of weakness. Nevertheless, reports of action initiated by Catholic institutions subsequent to the publication of the *Working Paper* suggest that the risk was well taken.

The Renewal of Catholic Higher Education is written with the same good will as was the *Working Paper.* However, the format is substantially different. To some, it may appear a step backward—that is, a retrenchment from the courage and forthrightness of the *Working Paper.* The Committee does not agree. The future development of Catholic colleges and universities will depend upon both the eradication of weaknesses and the continuation of programs and institutions that are already a source of pride. Consequently, the recommendations of *The Renewal of Catholic Higher Education* are based on a recognition of the immense diversity within Catholic higher education, on the very real and critical problems it now faces, and on its equally real and encouraging strengths. Although there has been much ado in the popular press about specific problems within Catholic institutions, the Advisory Committee is convinced that some of the most exciting developments in American higher education are taking place in Catholic colleges and universities. The guidelines suggested in this report are given with the hope that they will help encourage the added progress necessary to insure an effective future for Catholic higher education in the United States.

The Advisory Committee thanks its research staff for its efforts in helping to prepare a meaningful report. The members of the Committee express their gratitude also to the Fund for the Advancement of Education for funding this research project and to the hundreds of persons in Catholic colleges and universities who gave of their time and energy to answer questions, to provide data, and to offer suggestions and criticisms included in this report.

PREFACE

The description of Catholic higher education and the recommendations for its future developments contained in *The Renewal of Catholic Higher Education* are based on information gathered from five specific sources:

1. Institutional data provided to the Advisory Committee's research staff by Catholic colleges and universities through a survey form distributed in the fall of 1965.
2. Responses to an interview schedule administered on 98 Catholic college and university campuses during the academic year 1965-66.
3. Responses from major religious superiors to a questionnaire, distributed in the spring of 1966, dealing with accomplished, planned, or considered openings, discontinuances, or basic structural changes of Catholic colleges and universities.
4. Reactions in writing from Catholic educators to the *Working Paper,* privately distributed in the fall of 1966 by the Advisory Committee.
5. Comments, suggestions, and criticisms regarding Catholic higher education and, more specifically, the *Working Paper,* resulting from six meetings of the regional units of the College and University Department of the NCEA during 1966-67.

The Survey Form

In September, 1965, a survey form prepared by the research staff of the Advisory Committee was mailed to each of the 457 Catholic colleges and universities, including institutions conducted primarily for the education of religious men or women, as well as diocesan seminaries offering at least college level work. A total of 320 institutions (70%) cooperated by returning the requested information. Information was sought regarding the identification and location of the institutions, their control, admissions and enrollment, faculty, facilities, and financial support. The breakdown, by size and level, of institutions which completed the survey form is presented in Table 1.

TABLE 1

NUMBER AND PERCENTAGE OF INSTITUTIONS COMPLETING THE SURVEY FORM

		Total Number of Institutions	Number Completing	Percentage Completing
Level	I	131	75	57%
	II	230	171	74%
	III	78	60	77%
	IV	18	14	78%
Total		457	320	70%
Size Full-time Total Enrollment	Less Than 100	165	88	53%
	101 - 300	88	65	74%
	301 - 750	105	79	75%
	751 - 2,000	70	63	90%
	over 2,000	29	25	86%
Total		457	320	70%

The Interview Schedule

Although the information received from the colleges and universities through the survey form was highly useful and provided necessary and basic statistical information about Catholic higher education, the answers to certain questions and problems could not be made available through a written questionnaire. Since one of the main purposes of *The Renewal of Catholic Higher Education* is to provide a descriptive summary of Catholic higher education, it was decided that there would be no better source of information than those persons actually involved in the operation of Catholic colleges and universities. Through the cooperation of Dr. Manning M. Pattillo, Director of the Danforth Study of church-related institutions, an interview schedule was devised an administered on the campuses of 98 Catholic institutions. A total of 68 questions was asked of trustees, presidents, deans, development officers, librarians, faculty members, and students on each of the campuses. Among the major questions discussed during the course of the administration of the interview schedule were the following:

1. The distinctive role of that college or university not only as an independent institution but within a larger framework both Catholic and non-Catholic. Distinctiveness was sought through a series of questions dealing with institutional objectives, instructional programs, and extracurricular activities.
2. The particular relationship between the institution and other colleges and universities, the sponsoring religious order, and the diocese within which the college was located.
3. The predominant strengths and weaknesses of the institution as seen by those intimately connected with it.

The sequence of questions put to each particular group within the institution touched on similar topics; consequently, a series of checks and balances was established. Faculty members were asked to comment on the effectiveness of their own performance. They in turn, were "evaluated" by other groups within the institution. Students were asked to discuss their own concepts of the dedication and quality of the student body itself and also were the object of discussion by the other groups.

The main purpose of the interview schedule was to establish a general picture of certain qualitative dimensions within Catholic colleges and universities during the 1965-66 academic year. Since one of the major points of interest was the relationship existing either between or among Catholic colleges and universities located within a relatively short distance of one another, the method for selecting the institutions to be visited was based more on metropolitan area patterns of Catholic institutions than on selection of individual colleges or universities. The research staff visited metropolitan areas whose patterns of Catholic higher education differed. For instance, in one metropolitan area there may have been one large coed Catholic university, two or three Catholic women's colleges, a diocesan seminary, and several institutions devoted to the preparation of religious men or women. In another area, there may have been but one men's college and one women's college.

Several relatively isolated Catholic institutions were also visited since they represented another possible pattern. Table 2 gives a summary designated by the type of institutions visited.

TABLE 2

NUMBER AND PERCENTAGE OF CAMPUSES ON WHICH INTERVIEW SCHEDULE WAS ADMINISTERED

		Total Number of Institutions	Number Visited	Percentage Visited
Level	I	131	23	18%
	II	230	44	19%
	III	78	24	31%
	IV	18	7	39%
Total		457	98	21%
Size Full-Time Total	Less Than 100	165	24	15%
	101 - 300	88	10	11%
	301 - 750	105	26	25%
	750 - 2,000	70	25	36%
	over 2,000	29	13	45%
Total		457	98	21%

The Survey of Religious Superiors

In the spring of 1966 a questionnaire was distributed to the major religious superiors for men and to the major religious superiors for women. Approximately 800 of these questionnaires were mailed for information relative to the opening of Catholic colleges and universities, their discontinuance, and changes in control. Approximately one-half of the questionnaires were returned, but with relatively little information regarding either discontinuances that had occurred or plans to open or discontinue existing institutions. However, there was considerable comment by the major religious superiors on the problem of proliferation, a question specifically included in the questionnaire. The superiors also provided considerable information regarding the education of young religious. Statements of religious superiors regarding control and interinstitutional cooperation are incorporated in this report.

The Advisory Committee had distributed on a private basis 3,000 copies of its preliminary *Working Paper,* summarizing some of the principal problems confronting contemporary Catholic higher education. A page was provided in the *Working Paper* for reactions to the document. Approximately 100 persons responded. Their reactions, some of which were lengthy suggestions, are incorporated in this report. Through these reactions many specific examples of encouraging developments within Catholic colleges and universities were called to the attention of the Committee.

Response to Regional NCEA Meetings

During the academic year 1966-67, the research staff of the Advisory Committee attended the six regional meetings of the College and University Department of the NCEA. The main item on the agenda was a discussion of the *Working Paper.* The reactions of participants, their suggestions and criticisms were recorded by the research staff and are incorporated in this final report. Mention has already been made in the Foreword of the concern of many of the participants with the negative tone of the *Working Paper.* However, reaction was by no means predominantly critical. The Committee has attempted to include those criticisms and suggestions which seemed particularly meaningful.

CHAPTER ONE

Key Issues

Important to accurate interpretation of contemporary Catholic higher education, and critical for any suggestions about directions for its future, is recognition of both the great diversity in form and purpose of Catholic colleges and universities, and the fact that Catholic higher education is essentially a collection of institutions rather than a system or series of subsystems. The recognition reduces the risk of criticisms or guidelines based on inaccurate generalizations. Nevertheless, campus interviews and subsequent discussions at the regional meetings of the college and university department of the National Catholic Educational Association revealed substantial consensus among Catholic educators that there are areas of particular importance and special significance common to all Catholic institutions of higher education. Accurate information concerning these key issues was generally seen as essential to future development of Catholic higher education. The topics mentioned with the greatest frequency, and on that basis identified as key issues, were: financial support, the role of religious orders, planning and cooperation, and definition. Whether the issues are specifically Catholic or common to much of American higher education does not affect the validity of the statement that Catholic educators see the future of Catholic higher education as resting on the degree to which these issues on Catholic campuses will be honestly faced and decided.

Financial Support

Board members, administrators, and faculty consistently singled out inadequate financing as the most critical problem facing Catholic higher education today. It is their opinion that its future will depend more on the extent to which the institutions are successful in enlisting financial support than on any other variable. Interviewees saw lack of sufficient operational and capital income as the factor that has, above all others, kept Catholic institutions from realizing their full potential. It was also evident that all institutions find themselves in the same financial situation. The problem for some is the securing of income for future development and growth; for others, finding enough to make even continuation of current programs possible. Some institutions, to maintain competitive quality, "retrench" in size and level of offering if additional sources of income cannot be found. A few face decisions of closing. Only a very few indicated no serious concern at all about financing for the future.

Whatever the financial status of given institutions, all are being affected by some general trends in both income and expense. The two principal sources of income for the Catholic colleges and universities primarily for lay students come from tuition and fees and gifts from other than religious sources, that is, from parents, alumni, corporations, foundations, and friends. Again, because of the contributed services of religious, a form of indirect income, operational expenses in the Catholic colleges and universities have often been below what might be the case with non-Catholic institutions of similar size and level. Basically, the financial problem reduces itself to current trends in these three income sources.

Tuition rates have necessarily escalated on an almost annual basis to cover a constant percentage of operational costs. In fact, in many institutions, despite the "dangerously" high rate, the percentage of expenses which tuition income can cover continues to decrease. Many Catholic institutions feel they have reached the point where higher tuition rates would adversely affect either the size or complexion of the student body or both. Consequently, more and more operational income must be realized in the form of gifts, especially unrestricted gifts. Again, however, since all private institutions are feeling the financial pinch and since public higher education is turning more and more to the same gift sources, realistic but inadequate "ceilings" on gift income are facing many Catholic institutions. In short, many Catholic colleges and universities have now reached (or will soon reach) ceilings on their two principal income sources. This fact, together with ever-escalating expenses and the cost of competition, is putting a heavy tax on the ingenuity of financial officers.

The severity of the financial problem is intensified by two other facts directly involving religious personnel. The number of religious available or assigned to service in the colleges and universities and, consequently, the percentage of expense covered by contributed services have not kept pace with the manpower demands imposed by growth in size and complexity of the institutions. The recent trend to pay salaries to religious comparable to those paid their lay counterparts has aggravated the situation.

In general, then, the Catholic institutions facing the most serious financial crises are those in which tuition rates have reached competitive limits, expendable income from gifts has reached a ceiling, and the proportion of income realized through contributed services of religious has stabilized or dropped. This is the typical form that the financial crisis in a Catholic college or university is taking today.

Interviewees not only saw inadequate income as the major problem facing Catholic higher education but also agreed that this problem was generally felt at faculty, student, administrative, and physical plant levels.

The most critical adverse effect is the difficulty in recruiting and retaining superior faculties. Although there are in the Catholic institutions a large number of competent lay teachers who have resisted, and continue to resist, the enticements of higher salaries, more attractive fringe benefits, lighter teaching loads and increased prestige held out by more affluent institutions, their number cannot begin to fill the faculty ranks. Again, whereas in the past highly motivated Catholic scholars seemed convinced that the greatest contribution they could make to the Catholic effort in higher education was through work as a faculty member in one of the Catholic institutions, today they are attracted by the professional rewards and personal satisfaction open to them on secular campuses. Despite the almost impossible difficulties, the fact that some Catholic colleges and universities have managed to remain reasonably competitive in faculty salaries and the fact that a number of excellent scholars continue to bring both a deep sense of dedication and a high level of professional competence to Catholic campuses should be a source of great pride to Catholic higher education. This needs to be brought to the attention of the public as much as do some of the weaknesses of Catholic higher education.

Nonetheless, for the future, it would be unrealistic and selfish for Catholic institutions to expect any more than a handful of outstanding faculty to sacrifice financial and professional opportunities on other campuses simply because of an unselfish loyalty to Catholic colleges. In the future, the quality of the faculties in Catholic institutions will depend more on the provision of competitive salaries and benefits and less on the number of competent faculty willing to sacrifice professional advantages because of personal loyalty to Catholic institutions.

The effect of limited resources is felt by both the faculty and students. Many Catholic colleges reported that the proportion of resident students had increased much more in recent years than had been anticipated. This is traced to the fact that fewer and fewer local Catholic students can afford the higher tuition rates at the Catholic institutions. As a result of the emphasis in most Catholic colleges and universities on resident students, either national or regional competition, or both, has intensified for the better Catholic student. Most students who can afford to go to a local Catholic institution can also afford to go to a nonlocal one. The Catholic colleges thus find themselves in competition with an ever-widening circle of institutions for the students who are financially free to make a wide choice.

In addition to the problem of getting a sufficient number of students, the institutions are concerned with the effect of rising tuition rates on the socioeconomic make-up of the student body. Almost universally, presidents and deans regretted the meager funds available for scholarships.

Most institutions do not feel that they are getting their share of superior students or of low-income ones, especially from the disadvantaged sectors of the population. In both cases, the factor cited more than any other was lack of scholarship funds. Federal loan programs have enabled students from lower-income families to attend Catholic institutions, but these funds are not available in the amount needed to students from relatively well-to-do families and are not adequate to cover all costs for students from disadvantaged areas.

Again, in the colleges and universities which are badly in need of additional students, the danger of "floating" standards of admission has been noted. There is a tendency for more "exceptions" in the lean years. Administrators feel that the higher tuition rates and insufficient financial aid opportunities have frequently adversely affected the over-all quality of incoming students. Although this is by no means applicable universally to Catholic higher education, it is a problem in many Catholic institutions operating under severe financial limitations.

In addition to faculty and student problems, administration in Catholic colleges and universities has suffered from financial limitations. It is perhaps to the credit of administrators and boards that the operational funds available have generally gone first to support faculty and student welfare and then to supplement administrative services. But the policy also has serious disadvantages. Because of inadequate funding, top administrators typically have had to carry heavier workloads. Less than adequate time has been available to some of the potential leaders and spokesmen in Catholic higher education for creative thinking, planning and writing. As a result, much of the wisdom and experience of the best Catholic leadership has been hidden under a bushel. Again, because limited resources have precluded more extensive use of professionally prepared laymen in key administrative positions and because the pool of skilled administrators within any one religious community is relatively small, second-line administrators have been used. These often lack either the talent or expertise necessary to support the front line. Add to this the rapid expansion in both enrollment and complexity in many Catholic institutions, and you have a situation in which the institution has in some ways outgrown its management. Many problems could be alleviated if funds were available for both the personnel and facilities needed to support the general administration.

Finally, over and above the principal disadvantages caused by limitations on operational funds in Catholic colleges and universities are those which can be traced to lack of sufficient capital income. Although no institution is completely satisfied with the scope and condition of its physical plant, continued operation in the face of inadequate or substandard facilities can be extremely demoralizing. In instances where Catholic institutions have not been able to raise the necessary capital funds, the plant inadequacy tends to show up most frequently in substandard laboratory facilities and equipment; overcrowded or inadequate libraries; cramped or unattractive office space, particularly for the faculty; and insufficient provision of audio-visual equipment or of special educational devices.

Despite the general and serious problem of limited financial resources facing Catholic higher education, many Catholic institutions have had outstanding success in development campaigns. However, institutions which have raised large sums of money have frequently followed an inevitable trend to put too much of it proportionately into capital expenditures either for expansion or for replacement or worn-out facilities. Moreover, no matter what is raised and to what use it is put, the fact remains that it is still inadequate.

That high quality Catholic institutions find themselves critically in need of funds even though they have fully tapped available resources is a fact of American higher education that needs to be considered seriously by the American public. It is imperative to recognize that much of the criticism of Catholic colleges and universities could better be directed against a situation in American higher education that has put insurmountable limitation on those institutions and has undermined their inherent potential for excellence.

The Role of Religious Orders

A second key issue in Catholic higher education today is the question of the role of religious orders. Most Catholic colleges and universities in the United States were founded and have been nurtured by religious orders of men or women. As a result, what has been done and much of what is now being done in Catholic higher education is the result of efforts of members of one or more of the various religious orders of men and women. In the past two or three decades, there has been a tremendous growth in the numbers of laymen engaged in full-time work in Catholic colleges and universities. But, until quite recently, the religious have exercised the leadership and control, with the laymen "filling in" necessary gaps. Today the "dominance" of religious, while still a fact numerically at the administrative and governing levels in most Catholic colleges and universities, is being given close scrutiny, especially by the religious themselves. The reexamination of the role of religious in Catholic higher education is typically done in the context of questions of control, internal relationships between religious and lay personnel, and relationships between the Catholic colleges and universities and the hierarchy.

Boards of Trustees

Until very recently, Catholic colleges and universities sponsored by religious orders were governed almost exclusively by boards of trustees whose membership consisted either totally or predominantly of religious of the parent order. In some instances, most members were administrators or faculty of the institution itself; in others, officers of the General Provincial Administration predominated. There was little institutional representation. Almost universally, laymen constituted a minority. Lay "trustees" were usually members of an advisory board. However, recent changes in governing board structure at Saint Louis University, the University of Notre Dame, and University of Portland—all changes to heavy involvement of laymen—have generated considerable interest and controversy regarding the future role of religious orders in Catholic higher education. Questions are being asked about the canonical and civil law implications of such changes, as well as about the nature of ownership of a religious nonprofit organization. The phrase, "owned and operated by" (followed by the name of a religious order), is appearing less frequently in college catalogues. The phrase apparently is inconsistent with the true nature of a service corporation as a public trust.*

Although there is considerable interest in the type of change that has been made at the three universities mentioned above, it cannot be said at present that even a majority of Catholic colleges and universities are convinced that the change is for the best. More accurately it should be stated that Catholic educators see certain advantages and certain disadvantages relating to the change. Those who argue in favor of a change to governing boards of at least equal lay representation stress the disadvantages of so many Catholic college boards typical of the past, which were either exclusively or predominantly composed of members of the sponsoring religious orders. They argue that predominantly religious boards tended to reinforce the concept that Catholic higher education is primarily the responsibility of religious orders, rather than that of Catholics regardless of their particular state in life. The effect was to create an exaggerated possessiveness towards the institutions on the part of the orders and a "second-class citizenship" mentality among the laity. They also cite the fact that Catholic college boards of trustees have frequently been made up predominantly of religious who were concomitantly responsible for hospitals, high schools, elementary schools, and the motherhouse and a provincial seminary or both. They argue that such boards bring to decision-making a primary interest not in the institution but in the order itself, and this, more often than not, places the college in a disadvantageous position. Again, in the view of those advocating shared legal control, boards of trustees dominated by religious do not adequately or justly represent the various constituencies of the Catholic college or university, particularly business and civic groups. It is also argued that boards made up of both lay and religious

* (See Rev. John McGrath's study, *Catholic Institutions in the United States: Canonical and Civil Law Status,* The Catholic University of America Press, Washington, D.C., 1968.)

in approximately equal proportion will bring to matters of policy a wider range of talent and professional background and will insure a broader base for institutional financial support. Others, for more practical reasons, suggest that laymen can be expected neither to get deeply interested in a Catholic institution nor to give it the time needed if their role continues as that of advisory trustees.

On the other hand, many Catholic administrators see definite disadvantages to boards numerically dominated by laymen. They argue that while the disadvantages of boards dominated by religious typical of the past must be admitted, the weaknesses of such boards could be traced more to the fact that board members were not good trustees than to the fact that they were religious. To them the question whether a board member is a religious or not is irrelevant. Board members should be chosen on the basis of competence rather than according to a specific policy of proportional distribution. Further, some feel it is questionable whether there are yet enough laymen with either the understanding of the particular goals and nature of Catholic higher education or the professional experience to perform as competent board members. There is also the fear that lay boards of control in Catholic colleges and universities would ultimately result in a loss of Catholic identification. Still others are concerned that the public may easily misunderstand these changes, viewing them as a form of secularization, and mistakenly regard them as indications that the future of Catholic higher education lies in the direction of secularization. Finally, some institutions still rely on the parent religious corporation for financial stability, either by reason of greatly increased borrowing power for the institution or through actual subsidies from the parent corporation. In some instances a predominantly lay board, instead of enhancing the financial situation of an institution, may disrupt what financial stability has been there.

From the reaction of interviewees to the question of the constitution of membership of boards of control in Catholic colleges and universities, it is obvious that the institutions are seriously considering the pros and cons of changes in board membership. However, there was general consensus that each individual institution must make a decision appropriate to its unique financial, educational and manpower context, and that what may be best for one institution or one type of institution may not be best for another. There is no question, however, that the immediate future will see many and significant changes in the role of religious orders, particularly with regard to their involvement in the control of Catholic higher education. In sheer size and complexity, many Catholic institutions have reached the point of needing more than the resources of a single religious order or province if they are to continue to remain competitive in the future.

Internal Lay-Religious Relationships

It would be inaccurate to trace all the problems of faculty-administration relationships in Catholic institutions to causes other than those typical of any college or university. Nonetheless, because of the fact that Catholic college institutions have typically been controlled by a religious order and because of the fact that the percentage of laymen in key administrative positions has not kept pace with the percentage of laymen on the faculty, another dimension, that of lay-religious, has been added within Catholic colleges and universities to problems of faculty-administration relationships.

The real or apparent lay-religious dichotomy can be ascribed to several causes. Lack of adequate funds and the relatively small pool of laymen with necessary administrative talent or preparation account somewhat for the paucity of laymen in key administrative positions. Many problems are due to misunderstandings and lack of communication of various boards. Frequently an oligarchical or monarchical, rather than a democratic, tone has prevailed. The supposition that on a theoretical basis a single fiat from a religious superior could effect significant changes in even the most basic institutional policies has generated a feeling of insecurity among lay faculty. Actually, such fears have rarely been realized. However, this attitude on the part of the layman can be extremely demoralizing to an institution.

There have been instances also of conflicts between religious and laymen over the fact that a religious superior can assign to a given department of an institution a religious faculty member without first going through the channels customary for the appointment of a lay faculty member. Finally, the dominance of religious in administrative positions and on boards of control has often resulted in a hesitancy on the part of the lay faculty to become thoroughly committed to an institution which is seen in their eyes as belonging primarily to the religious order.

In fairness to the religious, it must be stated that they are not unaware of the problems that have been caused by the dominant role they have played in the administration and development of Catholic institutions. Again, where problems have developed between religious and laity, poor communication rather than poor policy has been found to be the cause in most instances. Currently there is great emphasis in Catholic institutions on formalizing procedures by which the lay faculty can participate appropriately in both governmental and policy determinations. More and more laymen are being appointed to high level administrative positions. Religious are more than willing to hand over to competent laymen administrative responsibilities when this can be done within the financial resources of the institution, and at such time as the religious are convinced that the layman does bring greater talent, knowledge and experience to the position. Both religious and lay interviewees emphasized the fact that what is desired in administration is the greatest possible effectiveness, and that appointment of officers should be based on professional competence, not on religious status.

Relationship of Institutions and the Catholic Hierarchy

An area of considerable mystery to those unfamiliar with the Catholic Church and of even more mystery to Catholics themselves, according to interviewees, is that of the relationship between a Catholic bishop and the Catholic colleges and universities in his diocese, particularly those controlled by exempt religious orders. All Catholic institutions, because they are Catholic, are under the general "pastoral" supervision of the local bishop. However, the degree to which bishops are involved in policy determination at the college or university level differs in the case of institutions sponsored by exempt religious orders and those sponsored by the diocese itself. The bishop is usually not a member of the board of trustees of those institutions run by religious orders. On the other hand, it is customary for the bishop to be chairman of the board of diocesan colleges and seminaries under his jurisdiction. In the latter instances, the bishop exercises a much greater role in policy determination and assumes larger responsibility for financial support of the institutions. From the point of view of civil law, the bishop exercises neither more nor less control over a diocesan institution than would be the case for any legal trustee. Because of the fact that he is generally a trustee in these institutions, he does have much more to say about their affairs than he does in the case of institutions run by exempt religious. With regard to the latter, the precise operational relationships between an institution and the bishop appear to be determined more by the particular interpretation the bishop puts on his responsibilities of general moral and pastoral supervision than upon any definitely prescribed rubrics. It is an admitted fact that friction has occurred and continues to occur between bishops and Catholic institutions of higher learning.

On the other hand, there are many examples of smooth relationships.* When trouble does occur, it can usually be traced in part to one or more of the following attitudes on the part of the institution controlled by the religious.

1. Dissatisfaction on the part of the institution with the apparent "disinterest" of the bishop implied in his relatively incidental interest in providing substantial capital or operational support.

2. An attitude on the part of the controlling religious order suggesting that the bishop is not sufficiently informed about

---

* (For an excellent and contemporary statement on true autonomy and academic freedom that should characterize a Catholic university see the report on *The Idea of the Catholic University* developed by a study committee of the International Federation of Catholic Universities and known as the Land O'Lakes Statement, 1967.)

the true mission or nature of an institution of higher learning, particularly the necessity of complete autonomy and freedom. Many of the tensions which exist between Catholic colleges and universities and bishops have resulted from actions of the bishop interpreted by the institutions as interference into what the latter consider internal affairs. The extent to which the bishop has either the obligation or the authority to legislate in matters pertaining to liturgical services on campus, speakers' policies, and theological requirements is a much disputed point and needs more explicit formulation.

3. Accusations from Catholic colleges and universities directed to the bishop which state that he has failed to encourage or demand more effective and meaningful long-range suprainstitutional planning at the college and university level. For example, a women's college becomes indignant over the fact that the bishop raised no serious objection to the decision of the local Catholic men's college to admit women—a move which the former saw as ultimately threatening its own existence.

The bishop faces a series of difficult dilemmas in dealing with the local Catholic college or university. Each dilemma becomes even more difficult in the case of institutions controlled by exempt orders. If the bishop sees it as his moral responsibility to question the institution about a certain liturgical practice or the appearance on campus of a highly controversial speaker, he is subjected to charges from the institution of undue ecclesiastical interference. If, on the other hand, he adopts a "hands-off" policy, he is frequently subjected to severe attack by local citizens, often representing various creeds. Moreover, frequently the parents of Catholic college students accuse him of contributing to the weakening of genuine morality or Christian conviction. Again, the bishop who recognizes the duplication of effort and the inefficiency and waste of money and manpower resulting from a proliferation of Catholic institutions of higher learning within his diocese often restrains from firm counteraction because of the risk of alienating one or more of the religious orders involved, whose members happen to staff other badly needed diocesan institutions.

Finally, in regard to the position to be taken on fund raising, the bishop is torn between allowing due freedom to each institution and the risk that in so doing he may create a disedifying and disabilitating interinstitutional competition.

There is no question that considerable attention needs to be given by Catholic higher education to the establishment of better communication and understanding between the hierarchy and the institutions. The need is imperative at the regional and national levels and within each diocese. At a time when all Catholic resources must be marshaled if Catholic higher education is to continue to be at all effective, the unnecessary and discouraging distance that has often existed between the hierarchy and the institutions must be corrected.

Planning and Cooperation

A third key in contemporary Catholic higher education, indeed in all American higher education, is that of planning and cooperation. To understand or to evaluate properly the status of cooperation, one must be concerned with the status of planning, for the level and effectiveness of cooperation parallel that of planning. Both planning and cooperation exist in Catholic higher education. However, both are circumscribed by a highly significant fact already emphasized—namely, that Catholic higher education is essentially a collection of institutions, a nominal category that happens to include a number of colleges and universities which declare themselves "Catholic." Whatever national, regional, or local planning exists among Catholic institutions, precisely as Catholic, has been effected only through voluntary and informal "associations" among the institutions themselves.

The first fact, therefore, about planning in Catholic higher education today is that, almost without exception, it is done at the institutional level. There is no agency, group, or organization in the structure of Catholic higher education itself which has legislative power at the national, regional, or local level as a vehicle for planning for cooperation. This may be surprising to one unfamiliar with the basic organizational structure of the Catholic Church itself, and particularly of those groups within the Church which have been most involved in the establishment, development, and operation of the Catholic colleges and universities—namely, the religious orders. Historically, the religious orders have enjoyed almost complete autonomy from the local bishop in matters of Catholic higher education. Although his permission has been necessary to found any Catholic college or university within his diocese and although he does have the authority indirectly to effect the discontinuation of any institution heavily dependent on members of a religious order by exercising his option of revoking permission for the given order to engage in activities within his docese, the bishop has seldom chosen to use this power. The bishops, therefore, are not in a position to "plan" Catholic higher education—either nationally, regionally, or at the diocesan level.

Again, each of the religious orders is autonomous. The Benedictines cannot legislate for the Jesuits, nor can the Sisters of Loretto do so for the Sisters of Mercy. Even within the larger religious orders themselves, there is no evidence of coordinated planning, except in the matter of distribution of personnel at the province level. Each college or university operates and develops as an individual entity rather than as a part of a larger system.

The national, regional, or local organizations which do exist within Catholic higher education, such as the National Catholic Educational Association or the Jesuit Educational Association, are voluntary associations, all seeking a greater unity of effort. The College and University Department and the seminary departments of the National Catholic Educational Association provide a forum for ideas, sponsor national and regional meetings, and offer some consultant and research services. Unfortunately, neither financial nor manpower support from participating institutions is sufficient to enable these departments to function as strong centralizing units. Regional associations of the various religious orders, while facilitating communication and performing various services, have only recently undertaken more intensive research and cooperative efforts. The Sister Formation Conference (which cuts across various religious orders) has indeed done much to break down the traditional insularity among religious orders of women and continues to encourage and effect greater coordination in that particular area of Catholic higher education. However, the Conference is by no means endorsed unanimously even by the orders of religious women themselves.

The fact that Catholic higher education is not a system and has been neither systematically planned nor controlled at the suprainstitutional level says nothing about either the advantages or disadvantages, or both, that have resulted from the fact. Indeed, interviewees saw both positive and negative effects emanating from the introduction of some form of extensive coordination into Catholic higher education. Some noted that at a time when the public sector of higher education is expressing concern over trends pointing to more sweeping federal and state control, and at a time when the monolithic state education systems are under severe criticism for losing sight of the value of the individual, the institutional freedom and individual autonomy of Catholic institutions and their independence from the regulations and determination of any system or subsystem appear to be a decided advantage. Again, the great diversity in form and function, the unique institutional interpretation of what it means to be a Catholic college or university, and the new experiments which spring from these conflicting interpretations would not be possible to the same degree if systematization were introduced.

Finally, the fact that each Catholic institution has stood its own merits and should be judged primarily on its own merits and performance has introduced what many view as a healthy element of competition among Catholic institutions themselves, a competition and an incentive for progress that might be lost in the case of centralization. On the other hand, many see disadvantages to the lack of systematization and suprainstitutional planning. Catholic institutions necessarily compete for a limited amount of total financial and manpower resources. The fact that Catholic colleges and universities almost universally list inadequate income as their major problem and the greatest impediment to growth in both size and quality and that many of these institutions have reached the limit of their financial potential is seen as an indication that total resources are spread too thin. Greater coordination and central planning could most certainly decrease the duplication of facilities, courses, general administrative expense, and personnel now characteristic of Catholic higher education in many metropolitan areas. The opportunities of a Catholic college education in any one region or area could be rationally planned rather than continue as the historical result of unrelated and uncoordinated foundings and developments. Again, the loss of potential in Catholic higher education that can be traced to lack of central assignment or distribution of resources is frequently criticized.

Apart from the interviewees' expression of arguments either for or against the introduction, either voluntary or imposed, of greater systematization and planning within Catholic higher education, there are conditions and trends affecting individual Catholic colleges and universities today that are generating active interest in the potential of greater coordination of effort. But there are also conditions and trends that *are* creating obstacles to coordination.

Many Catholic educators trace the history of relatively little cooperation among Catholic colleges and universities to the fact that these institutions, for the most part, have been essentially controlled by different and autonomous religious orders, among whom cooperation has certainly not been a traditional habit. The insularity of long years among religious orders, as well as among provinces within orders, has broken down considerably in recent years. The formation and encouraging work of the Conferences of Major Religious Superiors of men and of women evidence the fact. However, orders are only now beginning seriously to consider the possibilities of institutional mergers or other radical structural changes involving cooperation which would necessarily reduce the accustomed control and autonomy of individual religious orders. For many, the canonical and civil implications and difficulties implicit in corporate entities are still more awesome than the arguments for consolidation. On the other hand, as more and more Catholic institutions consider change toward boards of control whose membership is not predominantly composed of the religious of the sponsoring order, the possibilities of greater communication and involvement with other Catholic institutions are enhanced. Not a few interviewees see the trend toward "shared control" of Catholic institutions of higher learning as a possible prelude to basic structural changes within the local context of Catholic higher education. If it has been true that the basic argument for the continued existence of some neighboring Catholic institutions has been that of differences between religious orders, changes in control which reduce the position of dominance of a given order could well lead to meaningful consolidations or at least to more effective and substantial cooperation.

Although the academic arguments for greater institutional cooperation have always been strong, they seem to become much more cogent when reinforced by financial arguments or by necessity. Inadequate financial and manpower resources in Catholic higher education could hardly be called benefits, and they have been blamed as causes of most of the basic problems. Nonetheless, interviewees noted that some Catholic institutions in the process of undergoing serious financial crises have for the first time looked seriously to other Catholic or to non-Catholic institutions for solutions through cooperation. Although this may be neither the ideal motivation for cooperation nor a hopeful position from which to enter cooperative arrangements, it has in fact initiated cooperative ventures in instances in which academic arguments had proved relatively ineffective. The fact that the financial problems facing Catholic institutions seem to have neither an easy nor an immediate solution suggests that more and more interest will be generated in the potential interinstitutional cooperation of a substantial form.

In addition to the implications of changing patterns of control within institutions and the impetus of financial crises, the emphasis of the Second Vatican Council on the unity of the People of God and the basic responsibility of Christians everywhere to unite more effectively in a common Christian effort has undoubtedly generated in Catholic higher education considerable interest in genuine dialogue, both internal and external. This cannot but result in greater coordination. For example, some institutions, in looking to fundamental questions of what it is that makes the Catholic institution unique as an institution of higher learning and in searching for the arguments which ultimately justify continued existence, are recognizing that they have much more in common with other Catholic institutions than had previously been recognized. Differences between Jesuit and Dominican, between Presentation and Franciscan, while meaningful and necessary, appear less essentially divisive as the common Christian goals become more evident. Consequently, the possibilities of united effort become both attractive and possible.

Again, by stressing ecumenism, individual freedom and renewal, the Second Vatican Council has created on many Catholic campuses a climate for redefinition, for new experimental programs, and for exciting search for new interpretations of goals and strengths. While stimulating and encouraging, this search has created in many instances wider differences between neighboring Catholic institutions. Innovations seen by one institution as holding great potential for the future of higher education are eyed with suspicion by another. Institutions which see advantages in "deemphasizing" the Catholic element are viewed as giving up the fight by others who see the only hope for Catholic institutions lying in their specific "Catholic" uniqueness. The ecumenical spirit has led many Catholic institutions to explore new possibilities of cooperative arrangements with non-Catholic institutions. In fact, many interviewees saw the Second Vatican Council as being more valuable in bringing Catholic institutions closer to non-Catholic institutions than in creating a greater unity of effort among the Catholic institutions themselves.

Interviewees generally endorsed interinstitutional cooperation as holding tremendous potential for the future of Catholic higher education. However, it should be noted that despite the almost universal popularity, both within and outside Catholic higher education, of interinstitutional cooperation some interviewees viewed this emphasis as threatening rather than contributing to the future over-all improvement of Catholic higher education.

Although these strongly favor coordinated suprainstitutional planning, they argue that certain forms of interinstitutional cooperation may distract institutions from consideration of more radical solutions. They argue that the most serious weakness of Catholic higher education has been and still is the continued existence of Catholic institutions of questionable potential and effectiveness. They fear that a stress on the advantages of cooperation may encourage the institutions which should seriously be considering radical structural changes to carry on basically unchanged by using "superficial" cooperative devices of one form or another. In such cases, they argue, cooperation becomes but a crutch used to postpone more realistic, and possibly disturbing, decisions. It would be better not to encourage institutions to engage in cooperative efforts, they believe, if without such cooperation the institutions are basically unable to attain excellence. Interinstitutional cooperation should not be encouraged if there is no solid academic argument for continuing each of the cooperating institutions.

Proponents of this position suggest that Catholic higher education needs less interinstitutional cooperation and more structural consolidation. They are not opposed to the marshaling of resources. They argue instead that basic changes in structure, such as mergers or federations, would be much more effective toward this end than superficial cooperative exchanges. The basic purpose of cooperation is to create opportunities over and above those within reach of the cooperating institutions, and not to serve as a device for the perpetuation of individually inadequate institutions. Every institution should be able to offer a quality program consistent with its goals without intrinsic dependence on another institution. Although appearing severe and ruthless in their approach, those who discourage basically "superficial" cooperative programs are convinced that Catholic higher education as a whole would be better off if weaker institutions were to die a natural death rather than remain alive (but only marginally effective) either through mutual support or through the charity of more established institutions. The key question for an institution should not be: "With whom can we cooperate?" It should be: "Is our need for cooperation a symptom of basic inadequacy?"

Definition

The question of definition, or lack of definition, must be considered as one of the key issues in contemporary Catholic higher education. Indeed, many interviewees directly or indirectly stated that lack of adequate definition essentially underlies most, if not all, of the problems on Catholic campuses today, and that the answer to these problems lies more in arriving at meaningful definition than in anything else. They suggest that considerably more financial support would be given to Catholic institutions if potential benefactors were given a clear, functional definition of institutional goals and procedures, particularly those identifiable as "Catholic." Questions about the role of religious in higher education and about the relationships between Catholic institutions of higher learning and the Catholic Church itself reduce themselves basically to a matter of definition. Problems of academic freedom, of strained relationships between faculty and students, or faculty and administrators are seen basically as caused by inaccurate or uncommunicated concepts of the nature of a Catholic institution, and of the rights and duties of various groups within the institution. The lack of suprainstitutional coordination is seen also as being a result of the failure of individual institutions to define themselves as part of something larger.

Definition may or may not be the key issue in Catholic higher education today, but there is no question that interviewees saw it as a critical need. There were some differences of opinion, however, about the locus of definition. Some encouraged formulation at the national level, or possibly within similar groups of Catholic institutions, such as the large universities or the smaller women's colleges. Others, either because of the apparent hopelessness that a number of institutions could ever reach agreement or because of the immense diversity within Catholic higher education itself, favored definition at the institutional level. For a group of educators in any age to highlight definition as a critical need is not unusual. The history of higher education itself can easily and justifiably be interpreted as a continual search for definition. Why then is the need for definition in Catholic higher education any more critical today than it has been in the past? The reasons given by Catholic educators with greatest frequency are discussed below.

The Second Vatican Council has impelled Catholic educators to undertake an intensive reexamination of its implications for both the future form and function of Catholic institutions of higher learning. For example, the document on ecumenism suggests an examination of curricular patterns, particularly course sequences in theology, to determine whether students are being given the opportunity to learn and understand with some degree of adequacy points of view of religions and positions other than "their own." Although Catholic institutions have made use of non-Catholic theologians in the past, much more emphasis is being given now to provisions for broad and objective exposure to non-Catholic positions. In general, the document on ecumenism has emphasized the responsibility of the Catholic college or university to communicate more extensively and more openly with institutions and groups beyond the walls.

The redefinition and insistence of the Second Vatican Council on the concept of a united People of God is raising questions about whether Catholic institutions are fulfilling their responsibility of developing in their students and faculty a sense of responsibility for social involvement. The document on the apostolate of the laity has raised a number of questions. The traditional dominance of members of religious orders in both the control and administration of Catholic colleges and universities is getting a close look. Although the role of the laity in Catholic higher education has been changing for some years, the impact of the Second Vatican Council has intensified the question of the kinds of responsibility that can be expected of laymen at the college and university level. The document on religious freedom has raised very critical questions with regard to the extent and interpretation of academic freedom on the Catholic campus. Both the content and manner of presenting courses and the more general policies of faculty and students are being reexamined in the light of the emphasis of the Council on individual responsibility and freedom of conscience. The first reason for the need of definition within Catholic higher education comes, therefore, from the Catholic Church itself through the documents of the Second Vatican Council.

A second factor highlighting the need for definition in Catholic higher education is the current financial situation facing most Catholic colleges and universities. More and more of their support must come from outside gifts. Private corporations, key individuals, and the American public in general will not support these institutions to the extent that will be necessary unless they clearly understand the precise function of the Catholic institution and become convinced in growing numbers of the necessity of preserving such institutions in American higher education. Most Catholic administrators and faculty members seem convinced that the success of Catholic institutions of higher learning in getting their share of financial support will depend almost exclusively upon their success in arriving at precise and meaningful definition. This fact alone would make definition a critical need for the future.

Another factor necessitating definition within Catholic higher education is the all-too-frequent and widespread misunderstanding among the American public, and even among professional educators, of the basic purpose of the Catholic institution of higher learning and its relationship to the Catholic Church. Some of the recent articles in the popular press have caused considerable confusion. Isolated incidents have led to overgeneralizations. Too often the definitions presented by Catholic educators have been at best ambiguous and vague. Even with regard to very basic but important matters much of the American public is uninformed about Catholic higher education. There is little awareness that it is not a system, that Catholic institutions receive little direct support for operational purposes from church organizations. There is little understanding that the main purpose of a Catholic college or university is not to serve as an agent of the Catholic Church.

Pressures for definition come not only from sources outside the Catholic institutions themselves, but also from students and faculty. The increasing demands made by both student and faculty groups on administrators for clarification of function and roles are forcing a close examination of institutional policies, procedures and goals. There is now less passive internal acceptance of institutional definition and policy. As more and more Catholic colleges and universities prepare detailed, long-range projections and development plans, the need for precise operable definition becomes more apparent. It is impossible to project in detail 10-year needs and goals without a thorough understanding of the precise objectives to which the institution will be committed, as well as the specific means that will be employed to secure those objectives. Awareness is growing within institutions that too much of the definition of the past has been theoretical and abstract and too little of it operative. There has not been enough definition in terms of type and number of students, type and scope of programs, and sources and amounts of funding. There is little specific statement of how the institution's "Catholicity" translates itself into detail.*

There is then within Catholic higher education today wide recognition that definition stands as a key issue for the future. The need for precise and operative definition comes from the documents of the Second Vatican Council, the financial situation of most Catholic colleges and universities, misunderstandings among the American public and even among professional educators, internally from the students and faculty in the Catholic institutions, and finally from demands of intelligent long-range planning.

Apart from the need for more precise definition and the reason that it is critically needed, interviewees agreed in general on the areas or particular issues that required special clarification. Basically, they center on the question: "What is the meaning of 'Catholic' when prefixed to 'college' or 'university'?" The definition asked for is best outlined as that which would answer the following questions.

What kind of relationship to the Catholic Church itself is essentially established because a college or university calls itself "Catholic"?

Does a Catholic college or university shoulder, by the fact it is Catholic, greater responsibility for other Catholic colleges and universities and a larger picture of Catholic higher education than would a non-Catholic institution?

Is the relationship between a Catholic college or university and non-Catholic institutions any different than that among non-Catholic institutions themselves?

---

* The Washington Symposium on Catholic Education, sponsored by the NCEA in November, 1967, was at least a beginning of a nationwide cooperative effort to evaluate Catholic education in all its dimensions.

Is the "Catholicity" of a college or university curricular, co-curricular, extracurricular, or some combination of the three?

Does the "Catholicity" essentially necessitate faculty or student policies unlike those expected in non-Catholic institutions of higher learning?

Is it by student self-selection or by institutional intent that the "Catholic" college or university enrolls a predominantly Catholic student body?

Who should shoulder the legal responsibility for the continuation of Catholic colleges and universities in the future? the bishop? the bishops? the religious orders? laymen? Catholics?

The Catholic colleges and universities that have attempted to answer some or all of these questions evidenced in their answers the immense diversity of Catholic higher education. Nonetheless, whatever the possibilities of agreement among institutions, if each college or university was to set itself to the task of seeking answers to these questions, Catholic higher education would benefit immensely. It should be noted that interviewees sincerely thought that forthright answers to these questions would help American higher education appreciate to a greater extent the valuable contribution being made to higher learning in this country by Catholic insitutions.

The preceding paragraphs summarized the general consensus of interviewees of the need for definition in Catholic higher education today, of particular reasons for the need, and of several specific areas that need defining. The need for definition, then, has been widely recognized by Catholic institutions themselves. That relatively few have successfully formulated the desired definition cannot be traced primarily to unawareness of the need. The problem basically lies in the complexity of what is being defined, in the difficulty of arriving at consistency in definition, and in the problem of effective communication of definition once formulated.

Every Catholic college or university is an institution of higher learning, a public servant, a nonprofit corporation, a church-related institution, and a Catholic institution. Not only must definition be formulated from each of these points of reference, but each of the elements so described must be examined for consistency with each and all of the others. For instance, definition as an institution of higher learning must be consistent with definition as a Catholic institution. And precisely because the Catholic college or university has in some sense all of these characteristics, it is of vital interest to the general public, to professional educators, to professional societies, to local, state and federal legislatures, to foundations, to business corporations, to lawyers, to theologians, to bishops, to students, to faculty and to Catholic parents—to mention only a significant few. While it may be true that a Catholic bishop may be more interested in a Catholic college or university as a Catholic institution than as a public servant, and while a foundation may be more interested in the college and university as an institution of learning than as a church-related institution, the Catholic college or university does have the responsibility of trying to make as many of the publics knowledgeable about as many of the aspects of the institution as is possible.

Added to the difficulty of trying to define a basically complex entity with some consistency to a wide range of publics is the problem of the "level" and terminology of definition. Some definition must be abstract and philosophical, outlining basic principles or goals to which the institution is committed. Some must be more concrete and "operational." Problems arise when the philosophical does not easily become operable, or when apparent contradictions arise between the abstract and the concrete. Again, the language of definition may make sense to professional educators but mislead or misdirect the general public. What may satisfy the faculty may disturb the parents. The institution's interpretation of "Catholicity" may attract the liberal but scare the conservative. No more need be said to make the point of the enormous task the Catholic college or university faces as it moves toward more precise and meaningful definition. In conclusion, it should be noted that whereas interviewees saw solutions and definite steps to be taken by the Catholic college or university in certain problem areas such as the role of religious orders or interinstitutional cooperation, they offered few or not any suggestions for resolving the awesome problem of definition. The only agreed-upon suggestion as to how definition can be reached more effectively was that of broadening the base of formulation. If meaningful definition is to be achieved, it would seem to depend on the marshaling of ideas from board members, administrators, faculty and students, as these ideas form and reform through continuing internal and external communication. Definition cannot be left to a few Catholic leaders with the wisdom and courage to seek it. In fact, it would be accurate to state that interviewees in general expressed doubt that Catholic institutions could reach meaningful definition without help from Protestant, Orthodox, Jewish and secular sources. Besides, many interviewees suggested that those not directly associated with Catholic institutions may be more aware of the real values and the genuine contribution being made to American higher education by Catholic institutions than some of the Catholics themselves. Thus the inclusion of ecumenical insights in the search for definition might very well enable Catholic educators to relate Catholic higher education more surely and more delicately to the whole of higher education in America.

CHAPTER TWO

Recommendations

The recommendations that follow are implicitly contained in what Catholic higher education has said about itself in the facts described in this report. From conclusions of interviewees and respondents, the authors have selected only the most obvious and best substantiated recommendations.

Likewise, the recommendations for the future of Catholic higher education are directed primarily to the agents which control (or should control) that future—namely, the institutions themselves. Interested bishops, major superiors, involved religious, an available NCEA forum—none immediately shoulders or directs the future of individual Catholic institutions of higher education. That future lies in the action initiated by each institution itself. Nevertheless, this does not preclude the fact that outside the institutions—bishops, major superiors, etc.—will often be interested agents involved and/or affected by such action.

Just as no sweeping recommendations can be made for Catholic higher education as a whole, so no directives can be given for various types of Catholic colleges and universities. There is a strong temptation, for example, to recommend that no institution with fewer than 100 full-time students should continue to exist; that there should be no more than one Catholic women's college in any metropolitan area; that seminary education should no longer be done in isolation from larger institutions; that the large Catholic university should not try to maintain doctoral programs and professional schools in the face of the incomparable resources of public institutions. Not one of these recommendations could be made without reservations and conditions.

There are institutions for religious men and/or women with fewer than 100 full-time students which can be effective if creative use of full-time faculty is combined with meaningful and extensive association with neighboring institutions. There are instances in which more than one women's college should be continued in a metropolitan area because each offers an educational context of recognizable difference from the others. There are successful seminaries, particularly for the diocesan clergy, which for geographical reasons have had to operate without the opportunity of association with a larger university. There are Catholic universities which do maintain sound doctoral programs and have earned recognition for the quality of their professional schools. These institutions are committed for the future to the continued operation of this program level.

Specific types or groups of Catholic institutions must make policy decisions and take action on the knowledge of strengths, weaknesses and current trends within institutions similar to themselves.

The following recommendations are divided into two groups—institutional recommendations that pertain to the institutions as such, and collective recommendations that refer to colleges and universities as part of a local, regional, or national enterprise. A further division is made according to internal recommendations concerned with internal affairs and external recommendations concerned with external relations.

Internal Institutional Recommendations

1. Every Catholic institution of higher learning, as well as each of its constituencies—boards, administration, faculty, students—must recognize and exercise its responsibility for the quality of the institution.

> **This recommendation is implicit in the fact that there is no legislative or judicial suprainstitutional agency responsible for the quality of individual Catholic colleges or universities, precisely because they are Catholic.**

2. Each Catholic college or university should operationally interpret its "Catholicity." Specifically, the interpretation of "Catho-

lic" should enable the institution to resolve problems such as the following:

a) composition of board membership
b) choice of administrators and tone of administration
c) policies and procedures regarding selection and retention of faculty
d) faculty involvement in institutional decision-making and in policy formation
e) intellectual, socio economic, religious, and ethnic composition of the student body
f) sources and percentage of capital and operational income
g) curricular program(s)
h) cocurricular and extracurricular program(s)
i) student personnel policies

This recommendation is implicit in the fact that institutional definitions in Catholic higher education are frequently either vague or poorly communicated.

3. In addition to operational interpretation of the effect of its "Catholicity" on internal affairs, each Catholic college and/or university should interpret that Catholicity when it determines specific relationships with the Catholic Church itself and with the local hierarchy; relationships or joint responsibilities with other institutions of higher education—Catholic, Protestant, state, and secular; relations with government agencies—local, state or federal; relationships with a religious order.

4. There must be clear, effective procedures for involving outside agents in institutional definition, as well as honest, recurring intercommunication as definitions are formulated and reformulated.

Recommendations 3 and 4 are based on the fact that the effectiveness of definitions within Catholic higher education has been limited because interested external agents were not involved in the process of formulation or because the definition has been poorly communicated. As a result, agencies have been unable confidently and

intelligently to assess or determine their own behavior or attitudes toward the Catholic institutions.

5. Catholic institutions must honestly and courageously distinguish planning from dreaming. There must be honest, researched appraisal (institutional self-analysis) of present distance between goals and achievement, followed by realistic assessment of the probability of reducing that distance. In cases of low probability, radical change in goals or structures must be decided and implemented.

This recommendation is based on the fact that many Catholic institutions admitted a history and a future of questionable distance between stated goals and their realization.

6. Competent individuals must have the time and resources to "step back" from the institution in order to encourage and guide self-analysis and planning. There must be not only formal, clear, and effective procedures for involving board, administration, faculty, and students in the analysis and planning but also specific procedures for effective and continued intercommunication.

This recommendation is based on the fact that too few Catholic institutions have formal provisions for institutional self-analysis and long-range planning.

External Institutional Recommendations

7. Decision-making within Catholic colleges and universities must be done with responsibility. Decisions must be made with more than internal criteria in mind. The institution must face its responsibility for decisions that will strengthen, not weaken, other institutions.

This recommendation is based on two facts: (a) because of the lack of definition, understanding between Catholic institutions and "outside" Catholic and non-Catholic persons, groups, institutions and agencies is confused; and (b) too little responsibility has been exercised by Catholic institutions in weighing the effect of their policy decisions on other institutions.

Internal Collective Recommendations

8. Every Catholic college or university must recognize its unique responsibility to effect, maintain, and demonstrate the collective quality of Catholic higher education.

This recommendation is based on the fact that there is no legislative or judicial suprainstitutional agency responsible for the quality of Catholic higher education. The responsibility for the national, regional, or local status of Catholic higher education lies only with the institutions themselves.

9. Every Catholic institution should adopt an attitude of openness to possible avenues of coordination with other institutions, an openness free of predetermined limits. The degree and form of institutional autonomy should be determined only after (and not before) coordinated discussions are initiated.

10. The Catholic institutions within a given metropolitan or small geographic area should agree on a voluntary basis to conduct a professional feasibility study directed toward a creative answer to the question: "Given our combined financial and manpower resources, our existing and potential facilities, our special talents, what forms of structural organization would be most efficient and effective in accomplishing the goal of Catholic higher education in this area?"

11. If the feasibility study uncovers an exciting design, no matter how radical, the Catholic institutions must have the wisdom, courage and generosity to see to the implementation of the design.

Recommendations 9, 10 and, 11 are based on the fact that more coordinated planning is needed in Catholic higher education. Individual institutions acting in isolation cannot decide questions of possible proliferation and duplication, of more effective use of resources, etc. The most promising locus for greater coordination is at the metropolitan area level, rather than at the regional or national level. Whatever vehicles are set up for the purpose, they will be accepted by Catholic institutions only if voluntarily created by the institutions themselves.

External Collective Recommendations

12. Member institutions forming the College and University Department of the National Catholic Educational Association (NCEA) should promote the reorganization of that department into a well-financed agency specifically concerned with provision of the following services for Catholic higher education:

a) **Research services in all areas of concern facing Catholic institutions of higher learning. These services should be rendered from an expanded central office, as well as in coordination with a network of university-based higher education research and service centers concerned with the problem of all Catholic institutions of higher learning.**
b) **Consultation services for Catholic higher education. Such services can come from several areas—College and University Department of the NCEA, university-based research centers, sources of expertise within higher education as a whole but identified and supported by the NCEA College and University Department and directed to Catholic institutions of higher learning needing such consultation.**
c) **Published information service either in the form of a substantial and regular bulletin or in the provision of occasional papers directed to specific and timely questions faced by Catholic higher education.**

This tripartite recommendation is based on the fact that although the NCEA has had a long and distinguished history as a forum for discussion of the issues facing Catholic higher education, the NCEA College and University Department has not been developed as an effective service agency for the assistance of Catholic institutions of higher education.

13. The member institutions forming the NCEA College and University Department should, in conjunction with the implementation of recommendation 12 above, strengthen that department in a manner to allow for more effective representation to and communication with:

a) the National Conference of Catholic Bishops and individual members of the hierarchy;
b) the Conference of Major Superiors of Men and the Conference of Major Superiors of Women, allied agencies and individual religious orders;
c) agencies of the national, state and local government;
d) agencies and organizations which represent other segments of American higher education;
e) citizens in general regardless of creed and Catholic citizens in particular, since both in varying degrees are the recipients of the benefits of Catholic higher education and can be supportive of the enterprise of Catholic higher education.

This recommendation is based on the fact that Catholic higher education by its very nature as a collection of institutions of higher learning lacks a unified national agency that can represent the institutions with agencies concerned with American higher education.

CHAPTER THREE

The Institutions

Because Catholic higher education is an immense and very diverse enterprise, an examination of some basic facts about Catholic colleges and universities must precede any attempt to interpret or offer guidelines for this level of education. To ignore these facts invites distorted interpretation, provincial action and unfounded generalization.

In point of logical sequence the remaining chapters of this report actually precede the first two chapters. The chapters that follow provide the basic facts which document the key issues and give rise to the recommendations.

The Renewal of Catholic Higher Education deals with Catholic higher education and considers it as that educational effort in the United States represented by those institutions of higher learning sponsored by the Roman Catholic Church. It does not include the national Newman Foundation, hospital schools, or technical schools limited to professional preparation, except as these last two are part of the regular program of a degree-granting institution.

Not a System

Although it is possible to isolate 457 American institutions of higher learning under the general heading of Catholic higher education, this division is only a logical grouping. Catholic higher education is basically a collection of institutions which happen to be under the sponsorship of the Roman Catholic Church. It is not a system or an integral part of some larger system.

That Catholic institutions are all committed to or guided by the spiritual or intellectual ideals and values of the Catholic Church, that all are controlled by legal boards involving membership of religious men or women or by the clergy, and that the majority of students in the Catholic colleges and universities are Catholic—these facts make the Catholic enterprise in higher education no more a system than do certain factual characteristics which divide private from public colleges or junior colleges from four-year institutions.

For a group of institutions to be legitimately described or evaluated as an organic whole, they would have to be in some way centrally controlled and/or centrally planned or organized. To one unfamiliar with the organizational and governmental structure of the Catholic Church, it may be falsely assumed that Catholic institutions of higher learning are in whole or in part so managed. Nothing could be further from the truth. The individual colleges and universities under Catholic auspices are controlled by different religious orders or by different local dioceses, and all enjoy almost complete autonomy from other Catholic institutions.

Therefore, to avoid unwarranted criticisms and impractical guidelines, one must see Catholic higher education, not as a system, but basically as a grouping or collection of institutions.

Numerical and Percentage Distribution

The following tables provide information with regard to both the number and the percentage distribution of the Catholic institutions of higher learning in the United States for 1964-65.

Of interest is the discrepancy between the number of institutions (366) "controlled by Roman Catholic Church or Order" reported in the 1964-65 Education Directory of the United States Office of Education and the total (457) listed below. This discrepancy is due to the fact that some of the Catholic institutions do not meet the criteria for inclusion in the Office of Education Directory.

The discrepancy between the number of diocesan and religious seminaries reported in the Directory prepared by the Seminary Departments of the National Catholic Educational Association for 1965-66 (326) and the total reported below (126) is due to the fact that this present survey eliminated all seminaries below the collegiate level and those presently existing as extensions, divisions, or branches of larger institutions.

The tables do not include hospital schools of nursing or technical schools limited to one specialized field.

Classifications and Abbreviations

Level: The following four classifications by highest level of offering are used:

I. Two but less than four years of work beyond the 12th grade.
II. Only the bachelor's and/or first professional degree.
III. Master's and/or second professional degree.
IV. Doctor of philosophy and equivalent degrees.

Size: The following five classifications by size are used:

1. **Institutions whose total full-time enrollment was less than 100.**
2. **Institutions whose total full-time enrollment was more than 100 but less than 300.**
3. **Institutions whose total full-time enrollment was more than 300 but less than 750.**
4. **Institutions whose total full-time enrollment was more than 750 but less than 2,000.**
5. **Institutions whose total full-time enrollment was more than 2,000.**

Class: The following classifications by class (primary clientele) are used:

RM **Institutions operated primarily for members of one or more of the religious orders of men.**
RW **Institutions operated primarily for members of one or more of the religious orders of women.**
DC **Institutions operated primarily for members of the diocesan clergy.**
LM **Institutions operated primarily for laymen.**
LW **Institutions operated primarily for laywomen.**
C **Coeducational institutions.**
LT **Total number (or percentage) of institutions operated primarily for the laity.**
GT **Grand total.**

Age: The following two classifications by age are used:

Pre 1950—Institutions whose first class was admitted prior to and including the academic year 1949-50.

Post 1950—Institutions whose first class was admitted subsequent to the academic year 1949-50.

Regional Accreditation: The following two classifications by regional accreditation are used:

Accredited—Institutions accredited by one or more of the regional accrediting associations.

Non-accredited—Institutions not accredited by one or more of the regional accrediting associations.

Overall Distribution

Table 3 presents the overall numerical distribution of the 457 Catholic institutions of higher learning by level, size, class and age. Table 4 translates the numbers into percentages. From the two tables, the reader is made aware immediately of the great diversity of Catholic higher education. Highlights of interest follow the tables.

HIGHLIGHTS—TABLES 3 AND 4

A. Of the 457 Catholic institutions of higher learning:

1. 200 (43.8%) were operated primarily for religious men, religious women, or diocesan clergy.
2. 165 (36.1%) had fewer than 100 full-time students. Eighteen (11%) of these 165 were run for lay students; the balance, for religious men, religious women or diocesan clergy.
3. 253 (56.4%) had fewer than 300 full-time students; 64 (25.37%) of these 253 were run for lay students.
4. 29 (6.3%) had more than 2,000 full-time students.
5. 230 (50.3%) awarded as the highest degree the bachelor's or first professional degree.
6. 18 (3.9%) awarded the doctorate.
7. 139 (30.4%) admitted their first students sometime after 1950.

B. If the 200 institutions run for religious or clergy are excluded, the Catholic colleges and universities represented 13% of all American institutions and 20% of the private. Including the religious institutions, the figures jump 20% and 31%, respectively.

C. Of the 139 institutions admitting their first students since 1950, all but three had fewer than 300 full-time students.

TABLE 3

Statistical Universe (Numerical Distribution) of Catholic Institutions of Higher Learning By Age, Primary Clientele, Level, and Size

		PRE 1950								POST 1950								TOTAL								
Level	Size	RM	RW	DC	LM	LW	C	LT	T	RM	RW	DC	LM	LW	C	LT	T	RM	RW	DC	LM	LW	C	LT	GT	Size
I	1	11	14	6		1	1	(2)	33	8	42	7	1	12	1	(14)	71	19	56	13	1	13	2	(16)	104	1
	2			4	1	6	2	(9)	13	1	2	2		4	2	(6)	11	1	2	6	1	10	4	(15)	24	2
	3						2	(2)	2					1		(1)	1					1	2	(3)	3	3
	4																									4
	5																									5
	Total	11	14	10	1	7	5	(13)	48	9	44	9	1	17	3	(21)	83	20	58	19	2	24	8	(34)	131	Total
II	1	18	7	4					29	12	3	1		1	1	(2)	18	30	10	5		1	1	(2)	47	1
	2	5	2	13		14	3	(17)	37	1	2	4	4	9		(13)	20	6	4	17	4	23	3	(30)	57	2
	3	2		1	7	50	10	(67)	70		1			5	6	(11)	12	2	1	1	7	55	16	(78)	82	3
	4			1	12	16	9	(37)	38				3			(3)	3			1	15	16	9	(40)	41	4
	5				3			(3)	3												3			(3)		5
	Total	25	9	19	22	80	22	(124)	177	13	6	5	7	15	7	(29)	53	38	15	24	29	95	29	(153)	230	Total
III	1	11		1					12									11		1					12	1
	2		1	3		1		(1)	5			1					1		1	4		1		(1)	6	2
	3			4	1	11	2	(14)	18					1		(1)	1			4	1	12	2	(15)	19	3
	4				10	9	6	(25)	25												10	9	6	(25)	25	4
	5				8		8	(16)	16												8	0	8	(16)	16	5
	Total	11	1	8	19	21	16	(56)	76			1		1		(1)	2	11	1	9	19	22	16	(57)	78	Total
IV	1	1							1	1							1	2							2	1
	2	1							1									1							1	2
	3			1					1											1					1	3
	4			1		1	2	(3)	4											1		1	2	(3)	4	4
	5				2		8	(10)	10												2		8	(10)	10	5
	Total	2		2	2	1	10	(13)	17	1							1	3		2	2	1	10	(13)	18	Total
Total	1	41	21	11		1	1	(2)	75	21	45	8	1	13	2	(16)	90	62	66	19	1	14	3	(18)	165	1
	2	6	3	20	1	21	5	(27)	56	2	4	7	4	13	2	(19)	32	8	7	27	5	34	7	(46)	88	2
	3	2		6	8	61	14	(83)	91		1			7	6	(13)	14	2	1	6	8	68	20	(96)	105	3
	4			2	22	26	17	(65)	67				3			(3)	3			2	25	26	17	(68)	70	4
	5				13		16	(29)	29												13		16	(29)	29	5
	Total	49	24	39	44	109	53	(206)	318	23	50	15	8	33	10	(51)	139	72	74	54	52	142	63	(257)	457	Total

TABLE 4

Statistical Universe (Percentage Distribution) of Catholic Institutions of Higher Learning By Age, Primary Clientele, Level, and Size

		PRE 1950								POST 1950								TOTAL							
Level	Size	RM	RW	DC	LM	LW	C	LT	T	RM	RW	DC	LM	LW	C	LT	T	RM	RW	DC	LM	LW	C	LT	GT
I	1	2.4	3.1	1.3		.2	.2	(.4)	7.2	1.8	9.2	1.5	.2	2.6	.2	(3.1)	15.5	4.2	12.3	2.8	.2	2.8	.4	(3.5)	22.8
	2			.9	.2	1.3	.4	(2.0)	2.8	.2	.4	.4		.9	.4	(1.3)	2.4	.2	.4	1.3	.2	2.2	.9	(3.3)	5.3
	3						.4	(.4)	.4					.2		(.2)	.2					.2	.4	(.7)	.7
	4																								
	5																								
	Total	2.4	3.1	2.2	.2	1.5	1.1	(2.8)	10.5	2.0	9.6	2.0	.2	3.7	.7	(4.6)	18.2	4.4	12.7	4.2	.4	5.3	1.8	(7.4)	28.7
II	1	3.9	1.5	.9					6.3	2.6	.7	.2		.2	.2	(.4)	3.9	6.6	2.2	1.1		.2	.2	(.4)	10.3
	2	1.1	.4	2.8		3.1	.7	(3.7)	8.1	.2	.4	.9	.9	2.0		(2.8)	4.4	1.3	.9	3.7	.9	5.0	.7	(6.6)	12.5
	3	.4		.2	1.5	10.9	2.2	(14.7)	15.3		.2			1.1	1.3	(2.4)	2.6	.4	.2	.2	1.5	12.0	3.5	(17.1)	17.9
	4			.2	2.6	3.5	2.0	(8.1)	8.3				.7			(.7)	.7			.2	3.3	3.5	2.0	(8.8)	9.0
	5				.7			(.7)	.7												.7			(.7)	.7
	Total	5.5	1.9	4.2	4.8	17.5	4.8	(27.1)	38.7	2.8	1.3	1.1	1.5	3.3	1.5	(6.3)	11.6	8.3	3.3	5.3	6.3	20.8	6.3	(33.5)	50.3
III	1	2.4		.2					2.6									2.4	.2						2.6
	2		.2	.7		.2		(.2)	1.1			.2					.2		.2	.9			.2	(.2)	1.3
	3			.9	.2	2.4	.2	(3.1)	3.9					.2		(.2)	.2			.9	.2	2.6	.4	(3.3)	4.2
	4				2.2	2.0	1.3	(5.5)	5.5												2.2	2.0	1.3	(5.5)	5.5
	5				1.8		1.8	(3.6)	3.6												1.8		1.8	(3.5)	3.5
	Total	2.4	.2	1.8	4.2	4.6	3.6	(12.3)	16.6			.2		.2		(.2)	.4	2.4	.2	2.0	4.2	4.8	3.5	(12.5)	17.1
IV	1	.2							.2	.2							.2	.4							.4
	2	.2							.2									.2							.2
	3			.2					.2											.2					.2
	4			.2		.2	.4	(.7)	.9											.2		.2	.4	(.7)	.9
	5				.4		1.8	(2.2)	2.2												.4		1.8	(2.2)	2.2
	Total	.4		.4	.4	.2	2.2	(2.8)	3.7	.2							.2	.7		.4	.4	.2	2.2	(2.8)	3.9
Total	1	9.0	4.6	2.4		.2	.2	(.4)	16.4	4.6	9.8	1.8	.2	2.8	.4	(3.5)	19.7	13.6	14.4	4.2	.2	3.1	.7	(3.9)	36.1
	2	1.3	.7	4.4	.2	4.6	1.1	(5.9)	12.3	.4	.9	1.5	.9	2.8	.4	(4.2)	7.0	1.8	1.5	5.9	1.1	7.4	1.5	(10.1)	19.3
	3	.4		1.3	1.8	13.3	3.1	(18.2)	19.9		.2			1.5	1.3	(2.8)	3.1	.4	.2	1.3	1.8	14.9	4.4	(21.0)	23.0
	4			.4	4.8	5.7	3.7	(14.2)	14.7				.7			(.7)	.7			.4	5.5	5.7	3.7	(14.9)	15.3
	5				2.8		3.5	(6.3)	6.3												2.8		3.5	(6.3)	6.3
	Total	10.7	5.3	8.5	9.6	23.9	11.6	(45.0)	69.6	5.0	10.9	3.3	1.8	7.2	2.2	(11.2)	30.4	15.8	16.2	11.8	11.4	31.1	13.8	(56.2)	100.0

TABLE 5

Numerical and Percentage Breakdown by Level of American Colleges and Universities Which Were Catholic 1964-65

Level	ALL INSTITUTIONS				PRIVATE INSTITUTIONS			
	WITH SEMINARIES & SISTER FORMATION		*WITHOUT* SEMINARIES & SISTER FORMATION		*WITH* SEMINARIES & SISTER FORMATION		*WITHOUT* SEMINARIES & SISTER FORMATION	
	Number	Percentage Catholic	Number	Percentage Catholic	Number	Percentage Catholic	Number	Percentage Catholic
I	724	18%	627	5%	327	40%	230	15%
II	820	28%	743	20%	721	32%	644	24%
III	470	16%	449	13%	293	27%	272	21%
IV	224	8%	219	6%	117	15%	112	12%
Total	2238	21%	2038	12%	1458	31%	1258	20%

TABLE 6

Number and Percentage of Various Segments of American Higher Education by Level

Level	All Non-Catholic		Private Non-Catholic		Catholic Excluding Seminaries & Sister Formation		All Catholic	
	No.	Percentage	No.	Percentage	No.	Percentage	No.	Percentage
I	593	33%	196	20%	34	13%	131	29%
II	590	33%	491	48%	153	60%	230	50%
III	392	22%	215	22%	57	22%	78	17%
IV	206	12%	99	10%	13	5%	18	4%
Total	1781	100%	1001	100%	257	100%	457	100%

TABLE 7

NUMERICAL AND PERCENTAGE DISTRIBUTION FOR THE FOUR LEVELS BY REGIONAL ACCREDITATION, AGE, SIZE, AND CLASS, 1964-1965.

REGIONAL ACCREDITATION

Level	Total	Accred.		Not Accred.	
I	131	24	18%	107	82%
II	230	152	66%	78	34%
III	78	67	86%	11	14%
IV	18	18	100%	0	0%

AGE

Level	Total	Pre 1950		Post 1950	
I	131	48	37%	83	63%
II	230	177	77%	53	23%
III	78	76	97%	2	3%
IV	18	17	94%	1	6%

SIZE

Level	Total	1		2		3		4		5	
I	131	104	80%	24	18%	3	2%	0	0%	0	0%
II	230	47	20%	57	25%	82	36%	41	18%	3	1%
III	78	12	15%	6	8%	19	24%	25	32%	16	21%
IV	18	2	11%	1	6%	1	6%	4	22%	10	55%

CLASS

Level	Total	RM		RW		DC		LM		LW		C	
I	131	20	15%	58	44%	19	15%	2	2%	24	18%	8	6%
II	230	38	17%	15	6%	24	10%	29	13%	95	41%	29	13%
III	78	11	14%	1	1%	9	12%	19	24%	22	28%	16	21%
IV	18	3	17%	0	0%	2	11%	2	11%	1	5%	10	56%

HIGHLIGHTS—TABLES 5, 6, AND 7

A. The Level I Institutions

1. The percentage of all American Level I institutions represented by Catholic colleges and universities drops considerably (from 18% to 5%) if the seminaries and Sister formation colleges are excluded.
2. While one-third of all non-Catholic colleges and universities, and one-fifth of all non-Catholic private institutions of higher learning were junior colleges in 1964-65, only 13% of Catholic institutions run for the laity were Level I institutions. If seminaries and Sister formation colleges are included, however, the percentage for Catholic institutions was almost 30%.
3. 107 (82%) of the Catholic Level I institutions were not regionally accredited.
4. 83 (63%) of the Catholic Level I institutions admitted their first students since 1950.
5. 104 (80%) of the Catholic Level I institutions had less than 100 full-time students.
6. 58 (44%) of the Catholic Level I institutions were run for religious women.

B. The Level II Institutions

1. Both within Catholic higher education and in comparison of Catholic with other American institutions, the percentage of Catholic bachelor level institutions was the highest. For instance, (including seminaries and Sister formation colleges), while only 6% of all doctoral level American institutions were Catholic, Catholic institutions accounted for 28% of all American institutions at the bachelor's level.
2. The percentage of Catholic institutions which awarded only the bachelor's degree (60% for lay colleges, 50% of all) was higher than the percentage for either private non-Catholic institutions (48%) or the total group of non-Catholic institutions (33%). In fact, there were more Level II Catholic colleges and universities than there were any of the three other levels combined.

3. 78 (34%) of the Catholic Level II institutions were not accredited.
4. 53 (23%) of the Catholic Level II institutions admitted their first students since 1950.
5. 186 (81%) of the Catholic Level II institutions had fewer than 750 full-time students.
6. 95 (41%) of the Catholic Level II institutions were run for laywomen.

C. **The Level III Institutions**

1. The seminaries and Sister formation colleges improved the percentage of Catholic institutions at Level III. With these institutions included, Catholic colleges and universities accounted for 16% of all the American institutions classified at Level III, and 27% of all the private institutions at that level.
2. The distribution within Catholic higher education (lay colleges only) of Level III institutions was the same as that for the non-Catholic and the private non-Catholic groups.
3. 76 (97%) of the Catholic institutions at Level III admitted their first students before 1950.
4. 57 (47%) of these institutions were run for laywomen.

D. **The Level of Institutions**

1. In general, there were relatively fewer Catholic doctoral level institutions than was the case for the other groups of American higher education. If the seminaries were excluded, Catholic Level IV institutions represented only 6% of the Level IV institutions in the United States, and 12% of the private doctoral level institutions. If the seminaries are included, the percentage runs to 8% and 15%, respectively.
2. All of the Catholic doctoral level institutions are accredited.
3. The percentage of Catholic institutions awarding the doctorate (4%) was lower than that for either the total non-Catholic (12%) or the private non-Catholic (10%) groups.
4. 10 (55%) of the Level IV Catholic institutions had more than 2,000 full-time students.
5. 10 (56%) of the Catholic Level IV institutions were coed.

TABLE 8

NUMERICAL AND PERCENTAGE DISTRIBUTION FOR THE FIVE SIZE GROUPINGS BY REGIONAL ACCREDITATION, AGE, LEVEL, AND CLASS, 1964-65.

REGIONAL ACCREDITATION

Size	Total	Accred.		Not Accred.	
1	165	20	12%	145	88%
2	88	48	55%	40	45%
3	105	94	90%	11	10%
4	70	70	100%	0	0%
5	29	29	100%	0	0%

AGE

Size	Total	Pre 1950		Post 1950	
1	165	75	45%	90	55%
2	88	56	64%	32	36%
3	105	91	87%	14	13%
4	70	67	96%	3	4%
5	29	29	100%	0	0%

LEVEL

Size	Total	I		II		III		IV	
1	165	104	63%	47	28%	12	7%	2	2%
2	88	24	27%	57	65%	6	7%	1	1%
3	105	3	3%	82	78%	19	18%	1	1%
4	70	0	0%	41	59%	25	38%	4	3%
5	29	0	0%	3	10%	16	55%	10	35%

CLASS

Size	Total	RM		RW		DC		LM		LW		C	
1	165	62	38%	66	40%	19	11%	1	.5%	14	8%	3	2.5%
2	88	8	9%	7	8%	27	31%	5	5%	34	39%	7	8%
3	105	2	2%	1	1%	6	6%	8	8%	68	65%	20	18%
4	70	0	0%	0	0%	2	3%	25	36%	26	37%	17	24%
5	29	0	0%	0	0%	0	0%	13	45%	0	0%	16	55%

Distribution by Size

Table 8 presents a breakdown of the 457 Catholic colleges and universities by size. The table is followed by highlights of special interest.

HIGHLIGHTS—TABLE 8

A. Less than 100 full-time students

1. There were 165 Catholic institutions with fewer than 100 fulltime students.
2. 145 (88%) of these were not regionally accredited.
3. 90 (55%) admitted their first students since 1950.
4. 104 (63%) were Level I institutions.
5. 147 (89%) were run primarily for religious men or women or diocesan clergy.

B. More than 100 and less than 300 full-time students

1. There were 88 (19%) Catholic institutions with between 101 and 300 full-time students.
2. 40 (45%) of these were not regionally accredited.
3. Approximately two-thirds of this size group admitted their first students before 1950.
4. 57 (65%) awarded only the bachelor or first professional degrees.
5. 34 (39%) were liberal arts colleges for women.

C. More than 300 and less than 750 full-time students

1. There were 105 (23%) Catholic institutions with between 301 and 750 full-time students.
2. 94 (90%) had regional accreditation.
3. 91 (87%) admitted their first students prior to 1950.
4. 82 (78%) awarded only the bachelor or first professional degrees.
5. 68 (65%) were liberal arts colleges for women.

D. More than 750 and less than 2,000 full-time students

1. There were 70 (15%) Catholic institutions with between 750 and 2,000 full-time students.
2. All of these institutions were regionally accredited.

3. 67 (96%) admitted their first students prior to 1950.
4. 25 (38%) were Level III institutions.

E. More than 2,000 full-time students

1. There were only 29 (6%) Catholic institutions with over 2,000 full-time students.
2. All of these institutions were regionally accredited.
3. All of these institutions admitted their first students prior to 1950.
4. 26 (90%) awarded either the master's or doctor's degrees.
5. 16 (55%) were coed; the balance were men's institutions.

Distribution by Class

In Tables 9, 10, and 11 information is presented relative to Catholic institutions according to class. Tables 9 and 10 provide some comparisons of distribution between the Catholic institutions and other American institutions of higher learning on a basis of coed, men's, and women's institutions. Table 11 presents the breakdown by the six classes for the Catholic group.

TABLE 9

NUMERICAL AND PERCENTAGE BREAKDOWN (BY MEN, WOMEN, COED) OF AMERICAN INSTITUTIONS WHICH ARE CATHOLIC

	All Institutions				Private Institutions			
	Including Religious		Excluding Religious		Including Religious		Excluding Religious	
	No.	% Cath.	No.	% Cath.	No.	% Cath.	No.	% Cath.
Men	280	63%	154	34%	264	67%	138	38%
Women	320	68%	246	58%	312	70%	238	60%
Coed	1638	4%	1638	4%	882	7%	882	7%
Total	2238	21%	2038	12%	1438	31%	1258	20%

HIGHLIGHTS—TABLES 9, 10, AND 11

A. Institutions for Men

1. If the institutions for religious men, for the diocesan clergy, and for laymen are combined (178), they represent 63% of all the men's institutions of higher learning in the United States, and 67% of all the private institutions for men.

2. While only 6% of all American institutions and 8% of all private institutions were run for men, the figure for the Catholic segment was 39%.

TABLE 10

NUMBER AND PERCENTAGE OF VARIOUS SEGMENTS OF AMERICAN HIGHER EDUCATION BY COED, MEN'S, WOMEN'S INSTITUTIONS 1964-65

	All Non-Catholic		Private Non-Catholic		Catholic Exclud. Religious		All Catholic	
	No.	%	No.	%	No.	%	No.	%
Men	102	6%	86	8%	52	20%	178	39%
Women	104	6%	96	10%	142	55%	216	47%
Coed	1575	88%	819	82%	63	25%	63	14%
Total	1721	100%	1001	100%	257	100%	457	100%

B. Institutions for Religious Men

1. Of the 72 institutions for religious men, 57 (79%) were not regionally accredited.
2. Two-thirds of these institutions opened before 1950.
3. Approximately 20% of these institutions offered either the master's or the doctor's degrees.
4. 62 (86%) of the institutions had less than 100 full-time students; only two had more than 300.

C. Diocesan Seminaries

1. 23 of the 54 diocesan seminaries (43%) had regional accreditation.
2. Over 72% (39) were founded before 1950.
3. 21% of the diocesan institutions (approximately the same as that for the institutions for religious men) offered either the master's or the doctor's degree.
4. 27 (51%) of the diocesan seminaries had between 101 and 300 full-time students.

TABLE 11

NUMERICAL AND PERCENTAGE DISTRIBUTION FOR SIX CLASSES BY REGIONAL ACCREDITATION, AGE, LEVEL, AND SIZE.

REGIONAL ACCREDITATION

Class	Total	Accred.		Not. Accred.	
RM	72	15	21%	57	79%
RW	74	9	14%	65	86%
DC	54	23	43%	31	57%
LM	52	47	90%	5	10%
LW	142	110	77%	32	23%
C	63	56	88%	7	12%

AGE

Class	Total	Pre 1950		Post 1950	
RM	72	49	68%	23	32%
RW	74	24	32%	50	68%
DC	54	39	72%	15	28%
LM	52	44	85%	8	15%
LW	142	109	77%	33	23%
C	63	53	84%	10	16%

LEVEL

Class	Total	I		II		III		IV	
RM	72	20	28%	38	53%	11	15%	3	4%
RW	74	58	78%	15	20%	1	2%	0	0%
DC	54	19	35%	24	44%	9	17%	2	4%
LM	52	2	4%	29	56%	19	36%	2	4%
LW	142	24	17%	95	67%	22	15%	1	1%
C	63	8	13%	29	46%	16	25%	10	16%

SIZE

Class	Total	1		2		3		4		5	
RM	72	62	86%	8	11%	2	3%	0	0%	0	0%
RW	74	66	89%	7	9%	1	2%	0	0%	0	0%
DC	54	19	35%	27	51%	6	11%	2	3%	0	0%
LM	52	1	2%	5	10%	8	15%	25	48%	13	25%
LW	142	14	10%	34	24%	68	48%	26	18%	0	0%
C	63	3	5%	7	11%	20	32%	17	27%	16	25%

D. Institutions for Laymen

1. Excluding the 126 institutions for religious men and diocesan clergy, the Catholic lay colleges for men represented 34% of the colleges for men in the United States and 38% of the private men's colleges.
2. While only 6% of all American institutions of higher learning and 8% of all private institutions were run for men, 20% of the Catholic colleges run for the laity were men's colleges.
3. All but five of the men's colleges were regionally accredited.
4. 44 (85%) of the institutions for laymen opened prior to 1950.
5. 40% awarded either the master's or doctor's degree. (With the exception of the coed institutions, this is the highest percentage for any of the Catholic groups.)
6. 38 (73%) of the institutions for laymen had over 750 full-time students. (This is the largest proportion for any of the six Catholic groups. One-fourth of the men's colleges enroll more than 2,000 full-time students.)

E. Institutions for Women

1. The Sister formation colleges and the Catholic women's colleges total 216 and represent 68% of all the women's colleges in the United States and 70% of the private women's colleges.
2. While only 6% of all American institutions of higher learning and 10% of all private institutions were run for women, the figures for the Catholic segment (including Sister formation colleges) was 47%.

F. Institutions for Religious Women (Sister Formation Colleges)

1. 66 of the 74 Sister formation colleges (89%) had fewer than 100 full-time students.
2. Approximately two-thirds were opened since 1950.
3. 65 of the 74 were not regionally accredited.
4. 58 (almost 80%) were junior colleges.

G. Institutions for Laywomen

1. Excluding the 74 Sister formation colleges, the Catholic colleges for women represented 58% of all the women's

colleges in the United States and 60% of the private women's colleges.

2. While only 6% of all the non-Catholic American institutions of higher learning and 10% of the non-Catholic private institutions were run for women, 55% of all the Catholic colleges run for the laity were women's colleges.
3. 110 (77%) of the Catholic women's colleges had regional accreditation.
4. 109 (77%) of the institutions opened before 1950.
5. Two-thirds of the women's colleges were bachelor level institutions.
6. 68 (almost one-half) of the women's colleges had between 300 and 750 full-time students. None enrolled more than 2,000 full-time students.

H. Coed Institutions

1. The Catholic coed colleges represented 4% of all the coed colleges and universities in the United States and 7% of the private coed institutions.
2. While 88% of all the non-Catholic institutions of higher learning and 82% of all the non-Catholic private institutions were coed, the figure for Catholic institutions was only 14%. If only the Catholic colleges run for the laity are considered, coed colleges made up 25% of that group.
3. 56 (88%) of the Catholic coed institutions were originally accredited.
4. 53 (84%) of the coed institutions were founded before 1950.
5. 26 (41%) of the coed colleges offered either the master's or doctor's degree. 10 (16%) offered the doctorate.
6. The coed institutions were quite diversified in size. They included some of the smallest Catholic institutions as well as the largest. Approximately one-fourth of the coed institutions enrolled more than 2,000 full-time students; 52% enrolled more than 750.

Distribution by Age

While the categories of level, size, and class represent natural groupings under which the diversity of Catholic higher education may be detailed, the dimension of age is included here for a different reason. Various critics have lamented the number of new small Catholic institutions which have been and continue to be opened at an alarming rate. Since this proliferation is a topic of concern and considerable debate, the information provided in Table 12 is presented as background for intelligent discussion of the question.

HIGHLIGHTS—TABLE 12

A. Institutions Founded Since 1950

1. 139 (30.4%) of the Catholic colleges and universities have been founded since 1950.
2. 115 (83%) of these institutions were not regionally accredited in 1964.
3. 83 of these institutions (60%) were Level I institutions. Only three awarded the master's degree.
4. While there was considerable diversity in size among the new institutions, the greater majority (65%) had fewer than 100 full-time students. Only three enrolled more than 750.
5. 50 (36%) of the institutions opened since 1950 were Sister formation colleges; 33 (24%) were run for laywomen. Most of these originally were Sister formation colleges.
6. Almost two-thirds of the institutions opened since 1950 were run primarily for religious.

B. Institutions Founded Before 1950

1. 318 (69.6%) of all the Catholic colleges and universities were founded before 1950.
2. 237 (75%) of these institutions had regional accreditation.
3. 93 (30%) of the older group awarded either the master's or doctor's degree.
4. The older institutions evidenced a great diversity in size. 75 (24%) had fewer than 100 full-time students; 96 (30%), more than 750.

TABLE 12

NUMERICAL AND PERCENTAGE DISTRIBUTION FOR THE TWO AGE GROUPINGS BY REGIONAL ACCREDITATION, LEVEL, SIZE, AND CLASS.

REGIONAL ACCREDITATION

Age	Total	Accred.		Not Accred.	
Pre 1950	318	237	75%	81	25%
Post 1950	139	24	17%	115	83%

LEVEL

Age	Total	I		II		III		IV	
Pre 1950	318	48	15%	177	55%	76	24%	17	6%
Post 1950	139	83	60%	53	38%	2	1.4%	1	.6%

SIZE

Age	Total	1		2		3		4		5	
Pre 1950	318	75	24%	56	17%	91	29%	67	21%	29	9%
Post 1950	139	90	65%	32	23%	14	10%	3	2%	0	0%

CLASS

Age	Total	RM		RW		DC		LM		LW		C	
Pre 1950	318	49	15%	24	8%	39	12%	44	14%	109	34%	53	17%
Post 1950	139	23	17%	50	36%	15	11%	8	5%	33	24%	10	7%

TABLE 13

NUMERICAL AND PERCENTAGE DISTRIBUTION FOR THE ACCREDITED AND NON ACCREDITED GROUPINGS BY AGE, LEVEL, SIZE, AND CLASS.

		AGE			
Reg. Accred.	Total	Pre 1950		Post 1950	
Accred.	261	237	91%	24	9%
Not Accred.	196	81	41%	115	59%

		LEVEL							
Reg. Accred.	Total	I		II		III		IV	
Accred.	261	24	9%	152	58%	67	26%	18	7%
Not Accred.	196	107	55%	78	40%	11	5%	0	0%

		SIZE									
Reg. Accred	Total	1		2		3		4		5	
Accred.	261	20	8%	48	18%	94	36%	70	27%	29	11%
Not Accred.	196	145	74%	40	20%	11	6%	0	0%	0	0%

		CLASS											
Reg. Accred.	Total	RM		RW		DC		LM		LW		C	
Accred.	261	15	6%	9	3%	23	9%	47	18%	111	43%	56	21%
Not Accred.	196	57	29%	65	33%	31	16%	5	3%	31	16%	7	3%

5. Approximately two-thirds of the older institutions were run for the laity.

Distribution by Regional Accreditation

While the preceding tables provide information with regard to regional accreditation, the latter has not been the base for distribution percentages. Table 13 provides information with regard to the distribution of Catholic colleges and universities by regional accreditation.

HIGHLIGHTS—TABLE 13

A. Accredited Institutions

1. 261 (57%) of the 457 Catholic colleges and universities were regionally accredited in 1964-65.
2. 237 (over 90%) of the accredited institutions were opened before 1950.
3. Only 20 (8%) of the accredited institutions had fewer than 100 full-time students.
4. Only 47 (18%) of the accredited institutions were run primarily for religious.

B. Non-accredited Institutions

1. 196 (43%) of the 457 Catholic colleges and universities were not regionally accredited in 1964-65.
2. 115 (59%) of the unaccredited institutions had opened since 1950.
3. 185 (95%) of the unaccredited institutions were either Level I or Level II institutions, with 107 (55%) at Level I.
4. 145 (74%) had fewer than 100 full-time students. None of the unaccredited institutions had more than 750.
5. 153 (78%) were run primarily for religious.

CHAPTER FOUR

Descriptions by Class

In the preceding chapter, attention was focused on the extensive diversity within Catholic higher education in terms of the relative number of institutions falling into certain size, class, and level categories. The data have indicated that there is diversity even within one of the particular categorical divisions. On the other hand, there are certain characteristics which are more typical of one category than another.

In the pages immediately following, the six classes of Catholic colleges and universities are separately discussed. The statistical information is taken from the reports of the institutions which completed the survey form. The sections on strengths, weaknesses and implications are based on remarks provided the research staff during the administration of the inverview schedule, as well as on subsequent observations provided in the written reactions to the *Working Paper* and the six regional NCEA meetings noted in the Preface. Each of the class vignettes helps to portray both the diversity and the similarities among the institutions in each of the classes.

The Institutions for Religious Men

Seventy-two (15.8%) of the Catholic colleges and universities in the United States in 1964-65 were operated exclusively or primarily for the education of the members of one or more of the religious orders for men. These 72 institutions represent only a portion of the religious seminaries listed in the Directory of Catholic Seminaries in the United States published by the Seminary Department of the National Catholic Educational Association. This is due to the exclusion here of institutions below college level and those directly affiliated with or an integral part of a larger institution. In some instances, the religious seminary was operated not only for the education of the young members of a particular religious order for men but also provided opportunities for the education of local diocesan clergy. The 72 institutions range from junior college level to institutions awarding the doctor's degree. The breakdown for religious seminaries by level and size is presented in Table 14.

TABLE 14

INSTITUTIONS FOR RELIGIOUS MEN
BY SIZE AND LEVEL

Full-Time Total Enrollment	0 - 100	101 - 350	351 - 750	Total
Level				
I	19	1	—	20
II	30	6	2	38
III	11	—	—	11
IV	2	1	—	3
Total	62	8	2	72

Table 14 shows that approximately one-half (53%) of the institutions for religious men offered the bachelor degree as the highest degree awarded. Slightly less than one in every five of the institutions awarded either the master's degree or the doctorate. The majority of the institutions (86%) were quite small, having full-time student enrollments of less than 100. Only two of the institutions had more than 350.

In the preceding chapter it was noted that 79% of the institutions for religious men were not regionally accredited. Interviews with the rectors and deans on seminary campuses revealed that in many instances the institutions had not applied for accreditation. Therefore, the statistics should not be interpreted as an indication that these seminaries have tried and failed to get regional accreditation. The fact is that for various reasons such accreditation has, in most instances, not been sought. Among the reasons most frequently mentioned by the administrators for not seeking accreditation was a conviction that the accrediting agencies were not in a position to make an accurate judgment about the quality of seminary education, since the latter represented a rather specific type of higher education not common to the rest of American higher education. Another reason for not seeking regional accreditation was the fact that in most instances the young seminarian continued his higher education in institutions controlled by his religious order, which readily accepted credits earned at the seminary. It should be pointed out, however, that there is a trend in the seminaries toward more frequent application for regional accreditation. This is at least partly due to the fact that younger seminarians who drop out of the seminary program have found it difficult to transfer credit for courses to other institutions. The lack of regional accreditation by the seminary presents a serious problem for the seminarian who does not go on to complete his seminary education.

It was also noted in the preceding chapter that 58% of the seminaries for religious men were founded before 1950. Less than half have been opened since that date. Interviewees on seminary campuses suggested that the future will see relatively few new seminaries because of the growing interest in association with larger institutions, both Catholic and non-Catholic, rather than in continuing the more isolated patterns of the past.

Control

Information provided by 23 institutions for religious men with regard to the size and structure of the board of trustees indicates that these institutions are fundamentally controlled by the sponsoring religious order. The median size of the governing board of trustees for the institutions reporting was five. Most typically the five would consist of one or two superiors of the sponsoring religious order or the province itself and three or four administrative officers or faculty members from the seminary. While no specific statistics were available as to the number of seminaries for religious men which were separately incorporated from the controlling religious order, interviews on seminary campuses uncovered instances of both. The question of separate incorporation continues to receive attention by major superiors.

Although laymen, through membership on the legal board, do participate in the governance of the Catholic institutions run for the laity, none of the seminaries reporting had laymen on the governing board. Further, while laymen, through membership on advisory boards of trustees, frequently serve the interests of the Catholic colleges conducted for the laity, an examination of the data provided by the seminaries reveals that approximately two-thirds of the seminaries did not make use of such boards. Of the one-third that did not have advisory boards, only four had laymen on the board. It may be said then that laymen did not in 1964-65 play an important role in the governance of institutions run for the education of religious men.

Table 15 presents quartile points for a number of basic statistical dimensions of the 23 institutions for religious men which completed the survey form distributed by the research staff. The data provide information both with regard to the point about which these institutions tended to cluster and the degree of diversity within the group. The information in Table 15 is discussed briefly in the following paragraphs.

TABLE 15

RELIGIOUS SEMINARIES
ENROLLMENT, FACULTY, FUNDS—QUARTILE POINTS

ENROLLMENT	1Q	MEDIAN	3Q
No. Full-Time Total, 1964-65	43	70	78
% Increase, Full-Time Undergrads, 1961-65	2%	12%	53%
FACULTY			
No. Full-Time Total	6	8	10
% Part-Time, 1964-65	0%	22%	41%
% (Full-Time) Lay, 1964-65	0%	0%	0%
% (Ranked Faculty) with Doctorate, 1964-65	24%	30%	40%
FUNDS			
Total Current Income, 1964-65 (Thousands)	90	135	231
% Tuition and fees	0%	8%	33%
% Endowment	0%	0%	1%
% Federal government	0%	0%	0%
% Gifts from relig. sources	29%	54%	89%
% Gifts *not* relig. sources	0%	7%	20%
Total Capital Funds, 1960-65 (Thousands)	138	624	2,300
% From religious sources	97%	100%	100%

Enrollment

In general, the enrollments in institutions for religious men are quite small. It is not surprising, therefore, to find that the estimated total full-time enrollment for all 72 institutions in 1964-65 was only 5,000. The median full-time enrollment for the 23 institutions reporting was 70 students. One-fourth of the group enrolled fewer than 36 students; another one-fourth, more than 78. While the 72 institutions for religious men represented 15.8% of the total number of Catholic institutions of higher learning, they enrolled an 1.8% of the estimated total number of full-time students in attendance at Catholic colleges and universities in 1964-65.

A comparison of the full-time undergraduate enrollment for each of the reporting institutions for 1964-65 with that of 1960-61 shows over the four years a median cumulative increase of 12%, or approximately 3% per year. One-third of the institutions had experienced a decline in full-time undergraduate enrollment during the four-year period, and one-half reported an average annual increase of 4% or less. On the other hand, 27% of the institutions realized an average annual increase of 15% or better. The data indicate that some of the religious seminaries have grown considerably, while others have seen their enrollments fall off in the four-year period. Enrollment in these institutions is, of course, directly related to the number of vocations to the religious life. This is not the place for speculations as to the future of the Catholic religious orders for men. There is evidence that some religious orders have to be seriously concerned with the implication of the recent drop in vocations, while others have not experienced any alarming decline or have even had encouraging growth.

Faculty

Because of the very small size of most of the religious seminaries, the faculties reported were also small. The estimated total number of 600 full-time faculty members teaching in the 72 institutions for religious men in 1964-65 would approximately equal the number in a single larger institution. This total of 600 represented

3.2% of the estimated total number of full-time faculty teaching in all Catholic colleges and universities. As to individual institutions, the median number of full-time faculty for the religious seminaries reporting was eight, with one-fourth of the institutions having fewer than six full-time faculty members. The median percentage of the total faculty which was part-time for the institutions reporting was 22%, with one-fourth of the institutions having no part-time faculty at all, and another one-fourth having a part-time percentage in excess of 40%. In general, there is not a heavy dependence in the religious seminaries on part-time faculty.

Noted above was the fact that laymen were little involved in the governance of the institutions for religious men. The same is true with regard to participation by the laity in the full-time teaching in these institutions. In three-fourths of the religious seminaries reporting, there were no full-time lay faculty members at all, with the highest full-time lay faculty percentage being 10%. It can be stated then that both control and staffing of the seminaries for religious men were almost exclusively in the hands of members of the controlling religious order.

For each of the six classes of Catholic colleges and universities, statistics were available with regard to the percentage of ranked faculty holding the doctorate. Since most of the institutions for religious men had programs heavily emphasizing philosophy and/or theology and since excellent qualifications for teaching these two fields may not necessarily include the doctor's degree, this ratio when applied to the religious seminaries loses what significance it may have in other institutions as one index of faculty strength. However, the ratio in the religious seminaries differs but slightly from the ratio in the other five classes of Catholic institutions. The median percentage of the ranked faculty holding the doctorate for the religious seminaries reporting was 30%. In one-fourth of the institutions it was below 25%; in another one-fourth, above 40%.

Current Income

Because the majority of full-time faculty in the religious seminaries were members of the controlling religious orders and received no cash salaries, the annual cost of operating these institutions was generally small. For the institutions reporting, the median current income for 1964-65 was only $135,000, with one-fourth of the institutions reporting less than $90,000, and only one-fourth requiring more than $200,000. (Contributed services of the religious staff were not included in these figures.) It is interesting to note that the estimated total current income for 1964-65 for the 72 institutions for religious men was $12,000,000, considerably below that of a single larger institution. Relative to the argument that the operation of the many small institutions for religious represents a drain on the money available to the rest of Catholic higher education, it may be pointed out that the estimated percentage of the total operational money spent by Catholic higher education which went to the institutions for religious men in 1964-65 was well in line with the percentage of full-time students being educated. The institutions for religious men enrolled 1.8% of the full-time students in Catholic colleges and universities and engaged approximately 3.2% of the full-time faculty. The comparable percentage for current income was 2.6%.

As to specific sources of current income, the single largest category for the institutions for religious men was money from religious sources usually in the form of gifts or cash subsidies from the religious orders or from the local diocese. The median percentage of the total annual current income coming from this source for the institutions reporting was 54%, with one-fourth of the institutions receiving less than one-third from this source and another one-fourth receiving as much as 90%. No other single income source or combination of sources approximated the amount coming from the orders of the diocese. Tuition represented but a very small proportion of the operational income, with the median from this source reported as only 8%. Income from endowment was negligible. Only one-fourth of the institutions reported more than 1% of their 1964-65 current income from endowment. None of the religious seminaries reporting received operational funds from the Federal government. Gifts from sources other than the sponsoring religious order or the diocese accounted for a median 7% of operational income, with one-fourth of the institutions reporting no income from such gifts and another one-fourth more than 20%. In summary, the largest single source of operational income for the religious seminaries was gifts or subsidies from the sponsoring religious order or the local diocese. Income from all other sources was minimal, except for the few institutions which received a sizable portion of their operational income from gifts from private sources which could not be called religious.

Capital Funds

While there does not appear to be an argument that the institutions for religious men are draining an undue share of operational income from other segments of Catholic higher education, there is some justification for the position that these 72 institutions do represent a financial drain in terms of the amount of capital funds raised. For the religious seminaries reporting, the median amount of capital funds received in the five-year period preceding 1965 was $625,000, or approximately $125,000 per year. While one-fourth of the institutions had raised less than $25,000 annually during that period, another one-fourth had succeeded in raising more than $460,000 per year. The telling figure is the $40,000,000 estimated total amount of capital funds raised by the 72 institutions for religious men over the five-year period, which represented slightly over 7% of the estimated total raised during the same five years by all Catholic colleges and universities. While the institutions for religious men enrolled only 1.8% of the full-time students in Catholic institutions in 1964-65, engaged only 3.2% of the total full-time faculty, and received approximately 2.6% of the operational money, the percentage of capital funds going to this segment of Catholic higher education was some 7.1%. If the capital funds raised over the last five years were combined with the total value of the plant investment represented by these 72 institutions, there would unquestionably be a disproportionate amount of capital investment in the religious seminaries.

As was the case for operational income, the greatest source of capital funds for the institutions for religious men came from the sponsoring religious order or from the diocese. The median percentage of capital funds coming from religious sources for the institutions reporting was 100%. Only one-fourth received less than 97% of their capital funds from such sources. However, whether the money for capital purposes came from the order of the diocese or from other gifts, it must be included in the amount of "Catholic money" expended on seminary education in the years immediately preceding 1965.

In addition to statistical information about the institutions for religious men, the reader may be interested in a summary of the problems, strengths and implications for the rest of Catholic higher education which are most typical of the religious seminaries. The summary is based on interviews with seminary personnel, on responses from major religious superiors and on comments by Catholic educators.

Problems

The fact that many of the religious seminaries are very small presents some serious academic difficulties that are not outweighed by the advantage of individual attention to the students on the part of the faculty. Basically, the problems are twofold: providing sufficient depth and breadth of course offering and providing adequate opportunities for the more talented students.

The programs of most of the religious seminaries have been heavily geared toward professional competence in philosophy and theology and have not stressed the secular disciplines. This does reduce the number of faculty essential to basic implementation of institutional goals. However, a full-time faculty of eight (the median for those institutions reporting) can hardly be expected to bring enough diversity of outlook or breadth of professional preparation to insure the degree of intellectual exposure expected in an institution of higher learning. Seminarians frequently complained that the faculty seemed unusually homogeneous (the majority of full-time faculty are typically members of the controlling religious order). While most religious orders select and train their best men for faculty positions in the seminaries, the circumstances implicit in smallness continue to impose troublesome academic limitations which cannot be overcome easily by even the most talented faculty.

A second problem directly related to small enrollment is that of providing programs geared to the individual interests and talents of the seminarians. Demands on the faculty would be impossible if tailored programs were introduced. Consequently, regardless of particular interest or abilities, the seminarians have been exposed to the same sequence of classes and courses. Difficulties obviously arise for both faculty and student. The faculty member is sorely taxed to find the classroom presentation which will not lose the students of lesser talent and simultaneously prove challenging to those of exceptional ability. Conversely, the poorer students often find course work an impossible struggle, while the more talented easily lose interest and enthusiasm.

Finding effective means to broaden the curricular programs is another problem area. The impact of the Second Vatican Council, with its emphasis on academic excellence in the training of priests and religious, has been considerable. However, the problems faced by the small seminary in moving from a rather specialized program in philosophy and/or theology to one affording sufficient opportunities for study of the other academic disciplines are not easily solved. Although not the only reason, this dilemma is largely responsible for the trend toward integration of seminaries with larger institutions.

Since the religious seminaries are controlled almost exclusively by members of the sponsoring religious order and since the habit of obedience is one of the first lessons of the young religious, there is a natural tendency for the decision-making process in the seminaries to be more autocratic than is the case in other institutions. Nor is this style entirely internal. Several seminary rectors suggested that detailed long-range planning was almost impossible because of the long tradition of decisions imposed by major religious superiors. Fortunately, both within the seminaries themselves and in the relationship of the religious orders to the seminaries, there is a very definite trend toward a reduction in the more typical autocratic patterns of the past.

Strengths

Although the problems outlined above suggest very definite weaknesses in contemporary institutions for religious men, there are some equally important strengths. Among those deserving particular mention are the outstanding abilities and academic qualifications of individual faculty members, the typical serious-mindedness existing in most seminaries, and the role these institutions have placed in the preparation of many of the leaders in Catholic higher education.

Because of the commitment and investment of the religious orders in the education of their young members, the men selected to teach in the seminaries are usually those in whom the order has considerable confidence and respect. In professional preparation and ability and in dedication to an often unglamorous assignment, the greater proportion of faculty members in these institutions are outstanding. The academic weaknesses of many of the seminaries are due more to size than to lack of faculty talent or interest.

Religious superiors and faculty members in the religious seminaries frequently cited the serious-mindedness of the young seminarians. By choice of vocation, these young men have committed themselves to a way of life that de-emphasizes some of the extracurricular activities and interests that tend to distract many college students. As a result, there is an unusual personal discipline and dedication to work typical of the student body of religious seminaries.

In addition to the talent and dedication of so many of the faculty and students in the religious seminaries, these institutions can legitimately pride themselves on the fact that they have produced many of the leaders in Catholic higher education. The role the members of religious orders for men have played in the founding and development of Catholic colleges and universities in the United States is a matter of history. Only recently have laymen taken on a greater share of this responsibility. Certain problems can be traced to the traditional close association of Catholic institutions of higher learning with the religious orders of men, but without this involvement there would have been few or none of the positive achievements. Although the later training of the men who went on to become faculty and administrators was often received either at larger Catholic institutions or at non-Catholic universities, these men owe much of their effectiveness to habits engendered in the early years of seminary training.

Implications for Catholic Higher Education

The problems and strengths of the institutions for religious men are not the direct concern of Catholic educators involved in the other phases of Catholic higher education, but there are reasons why the status and future of these seminaries should be of considerable concern to all. The total amount of cash income needed to keep the 72 independent institutions for religious men in operation from year to year is not out of proportion to the number of full-time students enrolled, but the money expended annually for capital improvements and equipment and the combined plant value of these institutions represents a sum whose present use can be questioned. Apart from undesirable duplication of facilities, there is no doubt that the larger Catholic colleges and universities desperately in need of qualified theologians could benefit immensely if the faculty of the neighboring religious seminaries were made available to them. If some of the 800 full-time faculty now teaching in the 72 religious seminaries were to become a part of the regular faculties of the larger Catholic institutions, the quality and breadth of instruction in the latter could not but benefit.

Finally, the need of the seminaries for expanded curricular programs imposes an obligation on the larger Catholic institutions. In the past, the neighboring larger Catholic college or university could excuse its relative lack of involvement with the seminary on the grounds that the goals of the two institutions were quite different. Today, with the emphasis of Vatican II on superior academic preparation of priests and religious and the emphasis on the seminary as an academic institution, the argument is untenable. It would appear that both the seminaries and the larger Catholic institutions would profit from creative patterns of cooperation and consolidation.

Institutions for Religious Women (Sister Formation Colleges)

Seventy-four (16.2%) of the Catholic colleges and universities in the United States in 1964-65 were institutions run primarily for religious women. The 74 did not include a number of women's colleges which recently moved from a primary clientele of Sisters to that of both Sisters and laywomen. Nor does it include those Sister formation houses or institutions which are actually an integral part of larger institutions.

The Sister formation colleges are all committed to the general goal of the intellectual, spiritual and cultural development of the young members of one or more of the religious orders for women. Some of the larger orders run several such institutions, one for each or almost each of its provinces. Beyond their common commitment to the education of Sisters, there is as much diversity as there is similarity among the 74 institutions. At least four typical arrangements for Sister formation can be identified:

1. A small (fewer than 50 full-time students) two or four-year college, not separately incorporated, located in relative isolation from other colleges and universitites on the motherhouse grounds.
2. A small, relatively isolated, two or four-year college, separately incorporated from the motherhouse.
3. A small two or four-year college with a working agreement (re: transfer of students, credits, or faculty) with a larger neighboring institution.
4. A larger two or four-year college combining students and resources of several different orders.

The breakdown of the 74 Sister formation colleges for 1964-65 by size and level is presented in Table 16.

Of the institutions operated primarily for Sisters, 58 (80%) were Level I institutions with fewer than 100 full-time students. The bachelor level institutions were also quite small. In fact, approximately 89% of all the Sister formation colleges had fewer than 100 full-time students. Only one of the institutions had an enrollment of more than 300 full-time students, while seven had between 101 and 300.

TABLE 16

DISTRIBUTION OF SISTER FORMATION COLLEGES BY LEVEL AND SIZE, 1964-65

	Full-Time Enrollment			
	0 - 100	101 - 300	301 - 750	Total
Level I	56	2	—	58
Level II	10	4	1	15
Level III	—	1	—	1
Level IV	—	—	—	—
Total	66	7	1	74

As was the case for the institutions for religious men, a large percentage of the Sister formation colleges are not regionally accredited. In 1964-65, of the 74 institutions 65 (86%) did not have such accreditation. Campus interviews revealed that the reasons for the low percentage which were given by the institutions for religious men held for the Sister formation colleges. Many of those responsible for these colleges are of the opinion that the accrediting associations cannot understand the peculiar spiritual and intellectual problems of the training of young religious women and consequently are not in a position to pass qualified judgment on the quality of the institutions. On the other hand, as was the case with the institutions for religious men, more and more problems are being created for the unaccredited Sister formation colleges because of the inability of the young Sisters to transfer credits from these institutions to the larger colleges and universities. As a result, there is a growing trend among the Sister formation colleges to apply for regional accreditation.

Of all the classes of Catholic institutions of higher learning, the group which evidenced the greatest percentage increase in numbers of institutions over the past 15 years has been the Sister formation colleges. More than two-thirds of the 74 institutions conducted for religious women have been founded since 1950. One of every three Catholic colleges founded since 1950 is still a Sister formation college, while several others which began as such are now functioning as small women's colleges.

Control

Again paralleling the religious seminaries, the Sister formation colleges made little use of laymen in the formal governance of the institutions. Only one of the colleges reporting had laymen on the governing board. These boards ranged in size from 3 to 14 members, with a median of 6. Interviews revealed a trend toward separate incorporation of the Sister formation college from the motherhouse itself. However, in many instances this has not yet been accomplished nor is it seen as desirable. Some religious orders for women are not at all convinced that separate incorporation is wise. Often the college depends almost entirely on the financial assets of the order for credit and collateral. In such cases, separate incorporation would leave the college in a tenuous financial position. Whether the college is separately incorporated or not, there is a very close association with the motherhouse. In instances of separate incorporation, the boards of both the motherhouse corporation and the Sister formation college frequently have the same nucleus. The college board is generally slightly larger because of the addition of two or three college administrators to the motherhouse corporation membership. It can be stated that the control of the vast majority of Sister formation colleges is exclusively in the hands of the controlling religious order. On the other hand, the Sister formation colleges have made use of laymen on advisory boards of trustees to a greater extent than have the institutions for religious men. Approximately 60% of the Sister formation colleges reporting had advisory boards ranging in size from 3 to 21 members, with a median of 6, and on two-thirds of these laymen constituted the majority. Indirectly, through their services on advisory boards laymen, therefore, did participate in the governance of the Sister formation colleges.

Table 17 presents quartile points for a number of statistical dimensions for the 33 institutions for religious women which completed the survey form distributed by the research staff. The data provide information both with regard to the point about which these institutions tend to cluster and the degree of diversity within the group. This information is discussed briefly in the paragraphs below.

TABLE 17

SISTER FORMATION COLLEGES
ENROLLMENT, FACULTY, FUNDS—QUARTILE POINTS

Enrollment	IQ	Median	3Q
Full-Time Total, 1964-65	26	37	57
% Increase, Full-Time Undergrad., 1961-65	–8%	5%	37%
Faculty			
Full-Time Total, 1964-65	2	4	7
% Faculty Part-Time, 1964-65	45%	67%	82%
% Full-Time Faculty Lay, 1964-65	0%	0%	0%
% Ranked Faculty with Doctorate, 1964-65	6%	23%	27%
Funds			
Total Current Income, 1964-65 (Thousands)	14	44	97
% Tuition and fees	0%	15%	77%
% Endowment	0%	0%	0%
% Federal Government	0%	0%	0%
% Gifts from Religious sources	0%	21%	82%
% Gifts, *not* Religious sources	1%	5%	9%
Total Capital Funds Raised, 1960-65 (Thousands)	53	210	774
% From Religious Sources	7%	64%	97%

Enrollment

It has already been noted several times that the great majority of Sister formation colleges are very small institutions. The estimated full-time total student body for the 74 Sister formation colleges in 1964-65 was only 3,500, approximately 1.2% of the total full-time student enrollment in all Catholic institutions of higher learning for that year. It may be recalled that the 74 Sister formation colleges represented 16.2% of the Catholic institutions. The percentage of full-time students being educated in these institutions, then, is far below the proportion of institutions represented.

Most of the Sister formation colleges are small, but some differences were noted. One-fourth of the institutions reporting had less than 25 full-time students each, with the median for the group reported at 37. However, two of the institutions reporting had over 250 full-time students. Comparing the full-time undergraduate enrollments for these institutions for 1964-65 with that for 1960-61, 43% had fewer students in 1964-65 than they did four years earlier. In fact, two-thirds of the institutions reporting had either seen a decline in their full-time undergraduate enrollment or had realized an increase of less than 3% annually. On the other hand, 20% of the institutions reporting had experienced an average annual increase of 20% or more.

Enrollment in the Sister formation colleges is directly related, of course, to the number of vocations to the religious life. Those orders which have had some difficulties in the recent past have experienced the declines, while the orders whose vocation picture has been either stable or exceptionally good have experienced the increases. Interviews revealed that while there may be some continuing problems with regard to vocations, most major superiors expect a leveling off process as adjustments are made within the orders, and they do not believe that vocations will continue to decline indefinitely.

Faculty

Because of the small size of the Sister formation colleges the total number of full-time faculty in these institutions was not great. The estimated total for the 74 institutions was 350, which represented slightly less than 2% of the full-time faculty in all of the Catholic institutions in 1964-65. The percentage was slightly above the 1.2% for full-time students. A rather disturbing fact is that in one-fourth of the institutions reporting, there were no more than two full-time faculty members; the median was four. The figures suggest that the percentage of part-time faculty in these institutions was unusually high. This is confirmed by the fact that one-fourth of the institutions reported part-time faculty percentages of greater than 80%. The median for the institutions reporting was 69%. Only one-fourth of the Sister formation colleges reported fewer part-time faculty than full-time. In general, the part-time percentages for the Sister formation colleges were considerably higher than for the institutions for religious men.

It has already been pointed out that laymen played very little part in the formal governance of the Sister formation colleges. This is also true with regard to full-time teaching. In over three-fourths of the institutions reporting, there were no full-time laymen on the teaching staff. It should be noted, however, that interviews with administrators in the Sister formation colleges revealed that the absence of full-time laymen on the faculties was not due to choice but simply to the fact that institutions of such small size could not support the salaries of competent full-time lay faculty. The presidents and deans of many of these institutions indicated that they would prefer to have several full-time lay faculty members, but the institution did not have the money to recruit or retain them.

The percentage of the ranked faculty holding the doctor's degree in Sister formation colleges in 1964-65 was slightly lower in general than it was for the religious seminaries. The median percentage for the institutions reporting was 23%. In one-fourth of the colleges less than 6% of the ranked faculty held the doctorate. On the other hand, in another 25% of the colleges more than one-third of the ranked faculty held this degree.

Current Income

As was anticipated from the small size of the Sister formation colleges, the amount of current income received by them in 1964-65 was minimal. For the institutions reporting, the median operational income figure for the year was $44,000. Only one-fourth of the institutions reported more than $150,000 per year. It must be kept in mind, however, that the value of contributed services of administration and faculty was not included.

In discussion of the institutions for religious men, it was noted that while some Catholic educators have expressed concern over the cost to Catholic higher education of operating so many small institutions, the actual amount of money expended annually for operations by these institutions was not out of proportion to the number of full-time students in attendance. This was also true for the Sister formation colleges. The estimated total current income for the 74 Sister formation colleges in 1964-65 was only $5,000,000, approximately 1.1% of the total for all Catholic institutions for that year, and in line with the 1.2% of full-time students enrolled in the Sister formation colleges.

With regard to the sources of operational income for the Sister formation colleges, the most significant was that of gifts from religious sources. This is money given the college by either the sponsoring religious order or the local diocese. The median amount of current income coming from this source in 1964-65 for the institutions reporting was 21%. In one-fourth of the institutions, over 80% of the operational income came from religious gifts.

The second most important source of funds was tuition. For the institutions reporting, the median percentage from tuition was 15%. In one-fourth of the institutions it was higher than 77%. On the other hand, in another one-fourth of the institutions there was no tuition income reported at all. The only other important source category for current funds was that of gifts other than from religious sources. The median from this source for the institutions reporting was 5%. One-fourth of the institutions realized more than 10% of their annual operating income from such gifts. As was true of the religious seminaries, both endowment income and funds from the federal government were insignificant.

Capital Funds

The amount of capital funds raised by the Sister formation colleges during the five-year period prior to 1964-65 is of interest. The median for the institutions reporting was $210,000. One-fourth of the institutions received less than $50,000 over the five years, whereas another 25% raised over $800,000 each during the same time period. The estimated total for the 74 Sister formation colleges was $250,000,000, which represented approximately 4.4% of the total received during that period by all Catholic institutions. As was true for the institutions for religious men, the percentage of captial funds going to these institutions was above the percentage of either the full-time students or the full-time faculty. While the argument that too much "Catholic money" is going into the support of the Sister formation colleges does not seem defensible from the point of view of operational expenses, complaint is justified in view of the figures for capital funds raised. If the plant value of the 74 institutions were also included in these data, the argument would be further strengthened.

The source of the capital funds for the Sister formation colleges was primarily the sponsoring religious order or the local diocese.

For the institutions reporting, the median percentage of the capital funds which came from religious sources was 64%. In over one-fourth of the institutions the entire total received came from such sources. It should be noted, however, that another one-fourth of the institutions got less than 10% of their capital funds from either the religious order or the diocese. In general, the Sister formation colleges did not receive as high a percentage of their capital funds from religious sources as did the institutions for religious men.

Typical Problems

The Sister formation colleges share some of the problems of the religious seminaries discussed in the preceding section. Academic limitations because of small enrollments and difficulties resulting from a traditionally autocratic style of decision-making are common in both types of institutions. However, while the religious seminaries tend to suffer from restricted curricular programs, the Sister formation colleges face a different curricular problem. Many of the seminaries have historically de-emphasized disciplines other than philosophy and theology. The Sister formation colleges, on the other hand, have been committed to a liberal arts program. To cover even the basic liberal arts subjects in an institution with less than 100 full-time students is obviously difficult. The heavy dependence of these institutions on part-time personnel is necessary to provide opportunities for the students in the many academic fields for which Sisters from the order have not been specially prepared or cannot be spared.

According to many religious superiors, the basic problem for the religious orders of women is that of finding an arrangement for the college education of the young Sisters that will provide the ideal opportunity for them to understand and grow in religious and community life, while at the same time avoiding the academic deficiencies to which the very small institution is so subject.

Strengths

While the problems faced by the Sister formation colleges must be honestly recognized, so also should their achievements and strengths.

The dedication and talent of both faculty and students generally found in religious seminaries are quite as typical in the Sister formation colleges. In addition, because of the effort that must be made to provide an adequate education for the Sisters, some of these institutions have developed interesting, and apparently effective, interdisciplinary programs and experimental approaches to curricular design.

Finally, there are encouraging signs that the traditional insularity of the various religious orders of women is breaking down, with a growing number of programs based on pooled resources. There is also a trend for the small Sister formation college to make increased use of neighboring larger institutions.

Implications for Catholic Higher Education

There are several reasons why the Sister formation colleges should not be overlooked by the rest of Catholic higher education. First of all, the money required to build and maintain facilities for these institutions must be counted in the total resources available to Catholic institutions of higher learning. The facts indicate that an undue share is going to the smaller institutions run for religious. Secondly, the number of talented and highly trained Sisters teaching in the Sister formation colleges adds substantially to the potential faculty available to Catholic colleges and universities. Larger institutions could well make use of many of these religious.

Finally, the emerging efforts of the various Sister formation colleges to seek new forms for educating young Sisters through greater interinstitutional cooperation could well serve as models for the sort of cooperation and consolidation needed across the board in Catholic higher education.

Interviews with major religious superiors revealed that responsibility for the excessive proliferation of very small Sister formation colleges does not rest with the religious orders for women alone. In many instances, the establishment of such a college was the last resort on the part of the sponsoring order. In one case, the religious had received neither support nor advice from the larger Catholic institution to which they had turned. In other cases, financial or geographic circumstances left little choice. Finding a solution to the problem of the higher education of Sisters is a need that cannot be ignored by Catholic higher education.

Institutions for Diocesan Clergy

The institutions for religious men and the diocesan seminaries are in many ways similar, but there are some general differences in goals, financing, size and control which justify separate discussion. The basic distinction between the two types of institutions is that the religious seminaries are run primarily for young members of one or more of the religious orders for men, while the diocesan seminaries are conducted primarily for the education of young diocesan priests. While it is true that some of the diocesan seminarians receive their seminary education in institutions run primarily for members of the religious orders for men, the greater proportion attends institutions run specifically for the diocesan clergy.

In most of these seminaries, the control, administration and staffing are in the hands of the diocese itself. In some cases, however, the diocese has contracted with a religious order for men to assume the responsibility for educating the young diocesan seminarians. This describes, then, institutions run primarily for the education of diocesan clergy, most of which are controlled, administered and staffed by members of the diocesan clergy, with a number of the institutions under the direction of a given religious order for men. In 1964-65, 54 of the 457 Catholic institutions of higher learning were diocesan seminaries. This total of 54 included only those institutions offering college level work and operating as relatively independent institutions. Those seminaries which were part of a larger institution were not included. The breakdown by level and size for the diocesan seminaries is presented in Table 18.

Forty-three (approximately 80%) of the diocesan seminaries offered nothing beyond the bachelor's degree. Nineteen of these 43 were Level I institutions. Only 11 of the 54 diocesan seminaries had programs at the master's or doctoral level. The diocesan and the religious seminaries were quite similar in the percentage for

TABLE 18

Distribution of Diocesan Seminaries
By Level and Size, 1964-65

	Full-Time Enrollment				
	0 - 100	101 - 300	301 - 750	751 - 2,000	Total
Level I	13	6	—	—	19
Level II	5	17	1	1	24
Level III	1	4	4	—	9
Level IV	—	—	1	1	2
Total	19	27	6	2	54

both groups offering work beyond the bachelor's degree. In size, however, there were some differences between the two types of institutions. While 86% of the religious seminaries enrolled fewer than 100 full-time students in 1964-65, only 35% of the diocesan seminaries fell into the size group of 101 to 300. Two of the diocesan seminaries had full-time enrollments in excess of 750. While the diocesan seminaries were on the whole somewhat larger than the religious seminaries, they were still, comparatively speaking, very small institutions.

With regard to regional accreditation, the diocesan seminaries showed a higher percentage of accredited institutions (43%) than did either the religious seminaries or the Sister formation colleges (21% and 14%, respectively). Again, it must be pointed out that in instances where there was no regional accreditation it should not be concluded that the institutions involved were not qualified for such accreditation. Accreditation had not been sought by some of the diocesan seminaries for the reasons mentioned in the discussion of the religious seminaries. On the other hand, interviewees revealed a trend toward application for regional accreditation.

With regard to the foundation dates of the diocesan seminaries, there is much more similarity to the religious seminaries than to the Sister formation colleges. Whereas approximately two-thirds of the Sister formation colleges have been founded since 1950, only 15 (28%) of the diocesan seminaries have been opened since that date. One reason for the difference is that the seminary education of young clergy assigned to a newly created diocese has been handled by established diocesan seminaries, while there has been a tendency for each new religious order of women or each new province to establish a separate college for the education of the young religious women. Interviews with administrators in diocesan seminaries also revealed that there has been a greater interest in interinstitutional cooperation among the diocesan seminaries than has been typical of either the religious seminaries or the Sister formation colleges. Dioceses have worked out arrangements whereby one institution provides the undergraduate and/or philosophical training and the other takes the responsibility for theological preparation. There is also a trend for diocesan seminaries to affiliate or merge with larger Catholic universities.

As to the governing boards of trustees of the diocesan seminaries, there was considerable diversity in size for the institutions reporting. The boards ranged from as small as three to as large as seventeen, with a median of eight. Four out of the 21 institutions reported laymen on the governing board. In two of these four institutions the laymen made up either one-half or a majority of the board. In all other institutions the membership was entirely clerical. In general, while laymen played a somewhat more frequent role in the governance of the diocesan seminaries than was true for the religious seminaries or the Sister formation colleges, their involvement was still very limited. With regard to participation by the laity in the governance of the diocesan seminaries through advisory boards of trustees, nine of 24 seminaries reported having advisory boards, but only three of these involved laymen. Consequently, in general, the laity were not used in an advisory capacity by the diocesan seminaries to the extent that was true of the Sister formation colleges.

Table 19 presents quartile points for a number of statistical dimensions for the 25 diocesan seminaries which completed the survey form distributed by the research staff. The data provide information regarding both the point about which these institutions tend to cluster and the degree of diversity within the group. This information is discussed briefly in the paragraphs below.

TABLE 19

DIOCESAN SEMINARIES
ENROLLMENT, FACULTY, FUNDS—QUARTILE POINTS

	1Q	Median	3Q
Enrollment			
Full-Time Total, 1964-65	117	193	387
% Increase Full-Time Undergrad. 1961-65	–10%	3%	11%
Faculty			
Full-Time Total, 1964-65	9	15	18
% Faculty Part-Time, 1964-65	18%	39%	53%
% Full-Time Faculty Lay, 1964-65	0%	0%	40%
% Ranked Faculty with Doctorate 1964-65	16%	43%	59%
Funds			
Total Current Income, 1964-65 (Thousands)	188	285	490
% Tuition fees	22%	33%	75%
% Endowment	0%	3%	19%
% Federal Government	0%	0%	0%
% Gifts from religious sources	1%	12%	66%
% Gifts, *not* religious sources	0%	10%	17%
Total Capital Funds Raised, 1960-65 (Thousands)	338	590	2,800
% from religious sources	5%	83%	100%

Enrollment

Table 18 showed that, while the diocesan seminaries tended to be somewhat larger than the religious seminaries, the group on the whole consisted of relatively small institutions. The estimated total full-time enrollment of the 54 diocesan seminaries in 1964-65 was 12,000, 4.3% of the full-time students enrolled in all Catholic colleges and universities for that year. The diocesan seminaries, therefore, represented 11.8% of the Catholic institutions of higher learning but enrolled only 4.3% of the full-time students. Again, the difference among the diocesan seminarians can be noted with regard to full-time enrollments. While approximately 25% of these institutions had fewer than 100 full-time students, another one-fourth had more than 400. The median full-time enrollment for the diocesan seminaries reporting was 193.

Noted in the sections on the religious seminaries and the Sister formation colleges was the fact that superiors are concerned with the drop in vocations to the religious life and with the number of young religious leaving orders. The same concern was evidenced by administrators and faculty of the diocesan seminaries. Data comparing the full-time enrollments for the diocesan seminaries for the year 1964-65 with that of 1960-61 provide a base for such concern. Forty-three percent of the diocesan seminaries reporting had experienced a decline in full-time undergraduate enrollment during that four year period. In fact, 80% of the institutions reporting had experienced either a decline or an increase of less than 3% per year. None of the institutions had experienced as much as a 15% average annual increase during the four-year period. The median cumulative percentage increase for the four years for the institutions reporting was but 3%, or less than a 1% annual average.

Faculty

The estimated number of full-time faculty teaching in the 54 diocesan seminaries in 1964-65 was 800, approximately 4.3% of the total number in all Catholic colleges and universities for that year. The 4.3% is identical to the estimated percentage of full-time students enrolled in the diocesan seminaries. Paralleling differences in enrollment, the size of the full-time faculty differed considerably among individual institutions. While the median for the institutions reporting was 15, 25% had fewer than nine full-time faculty members, while another one-fourth had more than 18. The same diversity was reported with regard to the percentage of part-time faculty in each of the institutions. While the median was 39%, in one-forth of the institutions the part-time percentage was less than 18%, and in another one-fourth it was above 50%.

Reference has been made to the fact that laymen were little involved in either the control or the teaching in the religious seminaries and the Sister formation colleges. This was also true for most of the diocesan seminaries. More specifically, the median percentage of laymen on the full-time faculties of the diocesan seminaries in 1964-65 was 0%. It is interesting to note, however, that in 25% of the diocesan seminaries reporting, the percentage of laymen on the full-time faculty was greater than 40%. While it is true then that for three-fourths of the diocesan seminaries, laymen play little part in either the control or staffing, in one-fourth of the institutions they were heavily involved in full-time teaching.

Reiterating the theme of diversity which runs through the institutions of any given class were data regarding the percentage of the ranked faculty in the diocesan seminaries who held the doctor's degree. The median percentage for the diocesan seminaries reporting was 43%. In one-fourth, however, it was less than 15%, and in another one-fourth, greater than 60%.

Current Income

The annual current income and expense for the diocesan seminaries, both individually and as a group, ran higher in general than it did for either the religious seminaries or the Sister formation colleges. This was due to the fact that diocesan seminaries on the whole were larger institutions and that a greater proportion of the full-time faculty in these institutions was paid cash salaries than was the case for the institutions for religious men and women. The median current income in 1964-65 for the diocesan seminaries reporting was $285,000. Twenty-five percent of the institutions reported current incomes for that year of less than $200,000 each, but another one-fourth had incomes in excess of $500,000. The estimated total for the 54 diocesan seminaries was $20,000,000, approximately 4.3% of the estimated amount for all Catholic colleges and universities for that year. This 4.3% is identical with both the percentage of full-time students in the diocesan seminaries and the percentage of full-time faculty.

The two principal sources of current income for the diocesan seminaries were tuition and fees and gifts from religious sources. The median percentage of the total current income for 1964-65 for the diocesan seminaries reporting coming from tuition and fees was 33%, higher than the figure for either the religious seminaries or the Sister formation colleges. However, there was again a great difference among the seminaries themselves. In one-fourth of the institutions, the percentage from that source was less than 22%, while in another 25% the percentage was greater than 75%. The diocesan seminaries generally rely more heavily on tuition and fees than do the religious seminaries because the sponsoring religious order often picks up the total bill for the young religious.

As to the specific percentages of current income coming from gifts from religious sources for the diocesan seminaries, the median for the institutions reporting was 12%. The questionnaire did not request a distinction between gifts from religious orders and those from diocesan sources. However, interviews revealed that most of the gifts coming to the diocesan seminaries came from the local diocese rather than from other religious sources. Although the median percentage of current income coming from gifts from religious sources for the diocesan seminaries was 12%, 25% of them reported that only 1% of the current income came from religious gifts, and one-fourth of the institutions reported gifts accounting for more than two-thirds of the total current income. This difference is largely due to the policy of the particular diocese with regard to the principal methods for financing the local seminary. When tuition and fees are fairly substantial, the portion represented by subsidies from the diocese is smaller.

Tuition, fees and gifts from religious sources represented the two principal sources of income in 1964-65 for the diocesan seminaries. Endowment income and federal funds were of little importance. As to endowment income, the median for the institutions reporting was a mere 3% of the annual total, with almost one-half of the institutions reporting no endowment income at all. However, several of the institutions did report income from this source as high as 20% of the total current income. None of the diocesan seminaries reporting for 1964-65 reported receiving income from federal sources for operational purposes. As to gifts coming from other than religious sources, the median percentage reported by the diocesan seminaries was 10%. Once again there were differences among institutions, as one-fourth reported no income at all from this source and another 25% reported receiving in excess of 17% of their total current income from gifts from other than religious sources.

Capital Funds

Noted in preceding sections was the fact that the religious seminaries and the Sister formation colleges received "more than their share" of capital funds going to Catholic higher education during the five-year period immediately preceding 1964-65. The percentage of all capital funds going to these institutions exceeded the percentage of all full-time students in Catholic institutions.

The estimated $40,000,000 in capital funds raised during the five years by the diocesan seminaries represented approximately 7.1% of the total amount raised by all Catholic colleges and universities during the same period. This 7.1% is again higher than the 4.3% of the full-time students being educated in the diocesan seminaries. It should be noted, however, that the disproportion between the percentage of total capital funds and the percentage of full-time students reported for the diocesan seminaries is not as great as it was for either the religious seminaries or the Sister formation colleges. As to the individual dioceses themselves, the median amount of capital funds raised during the five-year period preceding 1964-65 was $600,000, or approximately $120,000 per year. In one-fourth of the institutions reporting, the cumulative amount raised was less than $350,000. On the other hand, in another 25% of the institutions the cumulative total exceeded $2,800,000.

There was again considerable difference among the institutions with regard to the source of the capital funds raised. While 25% of the seminaries received less than 5% of their capital funds from church or religious sources, another one-fourth reported that all capital funds had come from church sources. In general, most of the capital funds raised for the diocesan seminaries did come from church sources. This is evidenced by a median percentage reported of 83%.

Problems

The typical problems facing the diocesan seminaries are not unlike those common to the religious seminaries. Both must find solutions to academic and financial problems imposed by the small size of most of the institutions. Both are making an effort to move away from a rather autocratic style of administration typical of the recent past. Future institutional planning is hindered by the traditional policy of locating final institutional decisions either in the provincial house or in the chancery.

However, the tendency is more pronounced for the diocesan seminaries toward a curricular emphasis on philosophy and theology as tools for later professional and priestly work rather than as academic disciplines. Because many of the religious orders for men have for years been involved directly in the control and staffing of both high schools and institutions of higher learning, there has been a deeper interest in and talent for the implementation of seminary curricula which are more academic-oriented. While many of the diocesan seminaries have recognized this disadvantage and are moving toward both a reorganization and a re-evaluation of curriculum programs, interviews still brought frequent complaints from diocesan seminarians that the curricular emphasis was unduly pragmatic.

Since it is to the administration that an institution must turn for academic leadership, among the principal problems facing the diocesan seminaries at the present time must be listed that of finding competent academic leadership. Many of the religious seminaries solve their problem by drawing on men who have had considerable experience in college and university work, but the diocesan seminaries frequently do not have this same opportunity. Most of the diocesan priests have been engaged in pastoral work. Only recently have they become more heavily involved in higher education. Consequently, the pool of diocesan clergy who have had either a formal academic background or experience in college and university work is not as large as it is for many of the religious order for men.

Strengths

In general, the faculties and student bodies of the diocesan seminaries share the virtues of dedication to work and seriousness of purpose previously listed as strengths of both the religious seminaries and the Sister formation colleges. It may be noted also that the median percentage of ranked faculty holding the doctorate (usually the S.T.D.) was higher in 1964-65 for the diocesan seminaries than it was for any of the other five classes of Catholic colleges and universities.

Further, the effort to avoid unnecessary establishment of new institutions must also be listed as a virtue of the diocesan seminaries in general. There has been more effective cooperation and coordination among dioceses in this regard than there has among the various religious orders of men or women. As a result, a smaller proportion of the diocesan seminaries falls into the "less than 100 full-time students" category.

Finally, there are many examples of new experimental programs being tested by the diocesan seminaries. The potential to these institutions of the new ecumenical emphasis is great and should be considered among the resources available to these institutions for the future.

Implications for Catholic Higher Education

Interviews with persons in both the diocesan seminaries and the other Catholic colleges and universities evidenced the fact that until recently there has been relatively little communication between the two groups. Some seminary rectors and faculty members suggested that there has been an annoying habit among the colleges and universities of overlooking the seminaries as academic institutions. One of the implications and needs of Catholic higher education today is to recognize its responsibility for greater involvement with the diocesan seminaries. It would appear that through better communication and more effective cooperation, the diocesan seminary and the Catholic college or university might alleviate the problem of the seminary to broaden its curriculum and the critical need of the college to recruit trained theologians. This is but one example of the benefits which could result from a closer relationship between the diocesan seminaries and the rest of Catholic higher education.

Institutions for Laymen

This and the two following sections deal with the Catholic colleges and universities run primarily for lay students. Reference in this section to the men's colleges and universities is understood to exclude those institutions run primarily for members of religious orders or for the diocesan clergy. The 52 men's institutions accounted for 11.4% of all Catholic colleges and universities in 1964-65. There were approximately one-half as many institutions for laymen as there were seminaries. Table 20 gives the numerical breakdown for the men's colleges and universities by level and size.

TABLE 20

Distribution of Men's Institutions (lay)
By Level and Size—1964-65

Full-Time Enrollment

	0 - 100	101 - 300	301 - 750	751 - 2000	2001+	Total
Level I	1	1	—	—	—	2
Level II	—	4	7	15	3	29
Level III	—	—	1	10	8	19
Level IV	—	—	—	—	2	2
Total	1	5	8	25	13	52

Although there were individual exceptions, the men's institutions as a group were larger than the women's colleges. Thirty-eight (73%) enrolled more than 750 full-time students for the academic year 1964-65. Over 25% of the men's institutions had more than 2,000 full-time students. It may also be noted from Table 20 that 40% of the men's institutions awarded at least the master's degree, a percentage higher than that for any of the other five classes of Catholic institutions.

The percentage of men's colleges and universities which had regional accreditation was also higher in 1964-65 than that for any of the other class groups. Forty-seven of the 52 institutions (90%) were accredited. Noteworthy also is the fact that a higher percentage of the men's institutions (81%) was founded before 1950 than was the case for any of the other class categories of Catholic institutions.

Information with regard to the size and structure of the governing boards of trustees for the men's institutions reporting indicated both considerable diversity among the institutions with regard to the size of the boards, and a much greater involvement of laymen in the formal governance of the institutions than was the case for any of the religious institutions. The governing boards for the colleges and universities run for men ranged in size from as few as 3 members to as many as 25, with a median of 9. One-half made use of laymen, who constituted the majority in two instances. It should be recalled that this information was for the academic year 1964-65. Since that time several of the men's colleges have moved from boards having no laymen or a minority of them to new structures in which the laymen constitute the majority. Interviews with trustees and administrators in the men's institutions indicated that the trend toward governing boards numerically dominated by laymen will continue. However, particularly with regard to some of the smaller institutions, trustees and administrators were not universal in their conviction that laymen should represent a majority.

Data from the men's institutions reporting indicated that over three-fourths had advisory boards and that in all but one instance laymen constituted the numerical majority on these boards. Again there was a considerable difference among the institutions in the size of the advisory board. Institutions reported boards with as few as six members to as many as 58, with a median of 25. As the men's colleges move toward greater use of laymen on governing boards, the function of the advisory board has changed. In some instances, such boards have been dropped altogether. In general, it can be stated that whereas in the recent past most of the control by laymen over the men's institutions had been indirect through membership on an advisory board, there is now greater formal and legal involvement of laymen through actual membership on the governing boards of trustees.

Table 21 presents quartile points for a number of statistical dimensions for the 45 institutions for laymen which completed the survey form distributed by the research staff. The data provide information both with regard to the point about which these institutions tend to cluster and the degree of diversity within the group. This information is discussed briefly in the paragraphs below.

Enrollment

As to the specific full-time enrollments and enrollment trends in the men's institutions for 1964-65 and the years immediately preceding, considerable diversity is again evidenced. A comparison of the number of first-time applications for the institutions in 1964-65 with the number for each institution in 1960-61 shows a median four-year percentage increase of some 30%, or approximately 8% per year. However, in 12% of the institutions there were fewer applications in 1964-65 than had been the case four years prior. On the other hand, in 20% of the institutions reporting, applications had risen during the four-year period at an average of some 15% per year. The men's institutions were fairly similar with regard to the percentage of applicants being admitted. In only 25% of the institutions was the figure lower than 43%, and in another one-fourth of the institutions it was higher than 58%. In general, however, there was a tendency for the percentage to approximate 45%. Most of the men's colleges and universities were accepting four or five of every ten first-time applicants in 1964-65.

TABLE 21

INSTITUTIONS FOR MEN (LAY)
ENROLLMENT, FACULTY, FUNDS—QUARTILE POINTS

	1Q	Median	3Q
Enrollment			
Full-Time Total 1964-65	796	1256	1996
Full-time Graduate 1964-65	10	26	100
Part-Time Graduate 1964-65	53	250	500
Summer Graduate 1965	40	300	450
% Increase Full-Time Undergrad., 1961-65	5%	18%	28%
Faculty			
Full-Time Total 1964-65	41	68	103
% Faculty Part-Time, 1964-65	15%	24%	36%
% Full-Time Faculty Lay, 1964-65	60%	69%	75%
% Ranked Faculty with Doctorate, 1964-65	27%	35%	42%
Funds			
Total Current Income 1964-65, Thousands)	969	1895	3138
% Tuition and fees	59%	80%	89%
% Endowment	0%	1%	2%
% Federal Government	0%	0%	1%
% Gifts from religious sources	0%	0%	3%
% Gifts, *not* religious sources	1%	3%	9%
Total Capital Funds, 1960-65 (Thousands)	532	1275	3490
% from Religious Sources	0%	0%	2%

As to full-time undergraduate enrollment trends during the four-year period, the median cumulative percentage increase for the institutions reporting was 18%, or an average of slightly over 4% annually. Ten of the institutions had experienced a decline in enrollment. On the other hand, approximately 10% of the institutions had realized a cumulative increase in the number of full-time undergraduates during the four-year period of 60% or greater, in excess of 15% per year. It is clear then that while some of the men's institutions had experienced problems both with a decrease in number of applications and with enrollment during the four-year period preceding 1964-65, others had experienced considerable increases. The median full-time enrollment for 1964-65 was 1256, with one-fourth of the institutions reporting less than 800 and another one-fourth more than 2000.

The estimated full-time total enrollment for the 52 men's colleges was 82,500, approximately 30% of the estimated total in all Catholic colleges and universities for 1964-65. The men's institutions represented only slightly over 10% of all Catholic institutions of higher learning, but they enrolled about one-third of all the full-time students.

Seventeen of the 21 men's institutions offering graduate work during 1964-65 reported information with regard to graduate enrollment. The data indicated both a large difference among the institutions in terms of the size of the graduate programs and less full-time than part-time or summer work. For the institutions reporting, the median number of full-time graduate students was only 26. Only 25% of the institutions had full-time graduate programs involving more than 100 full-time students. On the other hand, 25% of the institutions reporting had fewer than 10 full-time graduate students. It should be noted that two institutions did enroll more than 700 full-time graduate students. This compares to part-time enrollment figures showing a median for the institutions reporting of 250, with 25% of the institutions enrolling more than 500 part-time students. The figures for summer graduate work are quite similar to those for part-time. The median for the institutions reporting was 300, with 25% of the institutions enrolling more than 450 summer graduate students and 25% fewer than 40. Although some 40% of the men's colleges and universities offered master's degree work or higher, the number of full-time graduate students involved in these programs was much smaller than that percentage might suggest. The estimated total number of full-time graduate students in the men's colleges for 1964-65 was only 3,500.

Faculty

The estimated total number of full-time faculty teaching in the men's institutions in 1964-65 was 4,700, approximately 25% of the total number of full-time faculty estimated for all Catholic colleges and universities for that year. However, the size of the full-time faculty for each of the men's institutions differed considerably. The median for the institutions reporting was 68. However, in 25% of the institutions there were fewer than 41 full-time faculty members; in another 25% of the institutions there were more than 100. The percentage of part-time faculty also differed, with one-fourth of the institutions reporting less than 15% part-time, while in another 25% the part-time faculty represented over 36% of the total. The median for the institutions reporting was 24%. In general, the part-time percentage for the men's institutions was lower than it was for any other class grouping of Catholic institutions with the exception of the very large coed universities.

Laymen played a significant role in terms of full-time teaching in the men's institutions. In only 25% of those reporting was the percentage of the full-time faculty which was lay less than 60%. The median for the reporting group was 69%. In fact, in one-fourth of the institutions reporting more than three out of every four full-time faculty were lay.

With regard to the percentage of ranked faculty holding the doctorate there was again considerable difference among the men's institutions. The median for those reporting was 35%. However, in one-fourth of the institutions the percentage was greater than 40% and in another 25% less than 27%.

Current Income

Data regarding annual current income for the institutions run primarily for religious revealed considerable diversity among the institutions, a difference traced principally to their difference in size. This same difference was found among the men's institutions. The median amount of current income reported by the men's institutions in 1964-65 was $1,895,000. However, 25% of the institutions reporting realized operational incomes for that year of less than $1,000,000, and another one-fourth had current incomes in excess of $3,000,000.

The estimated total current income for 1964-65 for the 52 men's colleges combined was $142,000,000, approximately 31% of the estimated total for all Catholic colleges and universities for that year. The 31% is in line with the 29.4% of the estimated total full-time students being educated by the men's institutions.

The two primary sources of current income were tuition and fees and gifts coming from other than religious sources. Tuition and fees represented the heavier percentage. One-fourth of the institutions listed tuition and fees as accounting for over 90% of the total current income in 1964-65. The median percentage reported was 80%. It is interesting to note, however, that 25% of the institutions realized less than 60% of their current income from this source.

With regard to gifts from other than religious sources, the median was 3%. In one-fourth of the institutions, however, this source represented more than 10% of the total current income. Endowment, the federal government, and gifts from religious sources were relatively insignificant sources of income for most of the institutions. With regard to endowment income, the median percentage of the total current income for the institutions reporting was a mere 1%. In well over 30% of the institutions there was no endowment income at all. In fact, in only 25% of the institutions did endowment income represent more than 2% of the total operational income for 1964-65. As to funds from the federal government, less than one-half of the colleges reporting indicated funds from this source. In only one-fourth of the institutions reporting was the percentage of total income coming from the federal government about 1%. Compared with those institutions run primarily for religious, the men's institutions got relatively little of their operational income in the form of gifts from religious sources. Less than one-half of the institutions reporting listed income from this source at all. In only 25% of the institutions did gifts from religious sources make up greater than 3% of the total operational income for 1964-65.

It would be incorrect, however, to assume from this data that the various religious orders for men were making no financial contribution to the men's institutions. Although the colleges and universities were not receiving direct subsidies from the religious orders, in many of these institutions a heavy percentage of the top administrative personnel and a sizable portion of the full-time faculty were members of the sponsoring religious order who received no more than minimal salaries for their services. This form of indirect financial support from the religious orders was of immense importance to the institutions, even though it was not reported as gift income.

Capital Funds

The men's institutions enjoyed varying success in raising capital funds during the five-year period immediately preceding 1964-65. The median for the institutions reporting was $1,275,000. However, 25% of the institutions reporting raised less than $500,000 each during the five-year period, while another one-fourth of the institutions succeeded in raising more than $3,500,000 apiece. The estimated total amount raised by the 52 men's institutions combined during that five-year period was $110,000,000, approximately 19.7% of the estimated total raised during the same period for all Catholic colleges and universities. This does not compare favorably with the 29.4% figure representing the percentage of full-time students being educated in the men's institutions. In this sense, the men's institutions have not received their share of capital funds raised by Catholic institutions. In fact, these institutions as a group show the greatest disproportion between the percentage of full-time students being educated and the percentage of capital funds being received. It was pointed out in preceding sections that each of the three classes of institutions run for religious were raising more than their share of capital funds. The shortage is being felt to the greatest extent by the men's institutions. As to the source of capital funds, data indicate that only a small amount came from religious sources. Less than one-half of the institutions reporting received any capital funds from either the sponsoring religious orders or the local dioceses, and in only 25% of the institutions did the percentage coming from these sources exceed 2% of the total raised by the institution.

Problems

According to interviewees, particularly younger faculty members and students, one of the problems typical of the Catholic men's institutions can be traced ironically to their basic strength. Because there is a greater proportion of the men's colleges and universities having larger enrollments, more stable faculties, and relatively long histories of successful undergraduate preparation than do the women's colleges, they are less often the targets of criticism. Charges of proliferation, inadequate staffing and lack of professionalism have been leveled less frequently at the men's institutions. Not a few faculty members, while taking a justifiable pride in the accomplishments of these institutions, expressed concern over the academic effect of an undue sense of complacency frequently characteristic of the men's institutions. Programs tend to become habits, and creative innovation is not common. The tendency toward rigidity is reinforced by the course sequences and requirements traditionally expected by way of preparation for professional life—a goal to which most of the men's institutions are essentially committed. Some of the institutions explicitly stress the liberal arts, but most clearly set preparation for professional or graduate work as primary goals. The demands of particular professions or academic disciplines in terms of required courses or hours often necessitate sacrifice of formal time allotted the liberal arts. Faculty members see this specialization emphasis as a potential threat to a vibrant intellectual life, a view that was confirmed by many undergraduates themselves.

A second weakness attributed to the men's institutions, most frequently by administrators in other Catholic colleges, is their apparent reluctance to involve themselves in interinstitutional cooperation of a more than superficial character. Because the Catholic men's college in many areas is a "stronger institution" than the neighboring women's college (s), negotiations for cooperative programs, if opened, are usually on terms set by the former. The men's institutions tend to see cooperative arrangements with a women's college as one-sided devices whereby the latter use the resources of the former to plug staff deficiencies in certain academic areas. Obviously, no completely successful cooperative venture can rest on such a premise. Cooperation among Catholic institutions would now be a much more common phenomenon had the men's institutions not approached the bargaining table with a conviction of superiority.

Strengths

It was suggested that in the men's institutions the more typical problems stem from a basic position of strength. The statistical dimensions of even the "median" men's institution delineate a college with a full-time enrollment approaching 1500, a full-time faculty of 70, and annual current income of approximately $2,000,000. The institutions are usually efficiently managed and generate considerable faculty and student loyalty. Most of the institutions have had more than adequate success in getting their graduates into respected professional and graduate schools. The controlling religious order generally enjoys the respect and support of the civic community. These are typical strengths of the Catholic men's colleges and universities.

Implications for Catholic Higher Education

With the exception of the smaller colleges, the implications for Catholic higher education of the men's institutions are much the same as they are for the larger coed institutions. These are enumerated at the end of that chapter.

Institutions for Laywomen

In terms of the number of institutions, in 1964-65, the colleges run for laywomen represented the largest group of Catholic institutions, accounting for approximately a third (31%) of all Catholic colleges and universities and over one-half (55%) of those institutions run primarily for the laity. These Catholic women's colleges represented 58% of all the colleges for women in the United States (excluding Sister formation colleges), and 60% of the private. Table 22 shows the breakdown, for 1964-65, of the Catholic women's colleges by level and size.

TABLE 22

Distribution of Women's Colleges (Lay)
By Level & Size—1964-65

	Full-Time Enrollment				
	0 - 100	101 - 300	301 - 750	751 - 2000	Total
Level I	13	10	1	—	24
Level II	1	23	55	16	95
Level III	—	1	12	10	23
Level IV	—	—	—	—	—
Total	14	34	68	26	

Table 22 indicates the heavy concentration of bachelor level institutions (67%). Twenty-three offered master's programs, but there was heavy emphasis on part-time and summer students at the graduate level rather than on full-time ones. As to size, slightly over one-third (68) enrolled fewer than 300 full-time students, with about one-half having full-time enrollments of between 300 and 750.

Most of the Catholic colleges for women were under the control of one of the various religious orders for women. In the past the association between the religious order itself and the colleges was extremely close, frequently with no legal separation of governing boards, but the trend in the recent past has been toward separate incorporation of the college. However, in many cases the membership of the governing board of the college and the governing board of the motherhouse itself still have the same nucleus. Typically, the college board would consist of seven members, four of whom would be more directly associated with the motherhouse rather than with the college itself. The governing boards in the women's colleges varied considerably in size, with some having as few as four members and others having nearly 25. Although approximately one-fourth of the institutions reporting had laymen on the governing board, with one or two exceptions laymen were in the minority. About 90% of the colleges reporting made use of some form of advisory board of trustees, with membership ranging from 5 to 60 members. Approximately one-fourth of the advisory boards numbered more than 25 members, with a median of 18 for the group reporting. Almost without exception, the advisory boards of trustees were made up either exclusively or primarily of laymen. Interviews with governing trustees and administrators revealed a general interest in testing greater involvement of laymen on governing boards of trustees, with a de-emphasis of advisory boards except as public relations instruments.

Table 23 presents quartile points for a number of statistical dimensions for the 120 women's colleges which completed the survey form distributed by the research staff. The data provide information both with regard to the point about which these institutions tend to cluster and the degree of diversity within the group. This information is discussed briefly in the paragraphs below.

TABLE 23

COLLEGES FOR LAYWOMEN
ENROLLMENT, FACULTY, FUNDS—QUARTILE POINTS

	Q1	Median	Q3
Enrollment			
Full-Time Total, 1964-65	257	461	733
% Increase Full-Time Undergrad., 1961-65	12%	30%	51%
Full-Time Graduate, 1964-65	0	9	19
Part-Time Graduate, 1964-65	0	88	136
Summer Graduate, 1965	105	256	338
Faculty			
Full-Time Total, 1964-65	25	34	57
% Faculty Part-Time, 1964-65	23%	31%	39%
% Full-Time Faculty Lay, 1964-65	27%	40%	53%
% Ranked Faculty with Doctorate, 1964-65	18%	27%	31%
FUNDS			
Total Current Income, 1964-65 (Thousands)	384	721	1217
% Tuition and fees	46%	65%	80%
% Endowment	0%	1%	2%
% Federal Government	0%	0%	1%
% Gifts from religious sources	0%	0%	8%
% Gifts, *not* religious sources	3%	7%	15%
Total Capital Funds, 1960-65 (Thousands)	597	1016	2186
% Gifts From Religious Sources	0%	0%	56%

Enrollment

It has already been pointed out that the Catholic women's colleges tend to be smaller on the whole than either the men's colleges or the coed institutions. However, within the women's group itself, there was a considerable difference in the sizes of the colleges in 1964-65. While one-fourth of those reporting had fewer than 250 full-time students, another 25% enrolled more than 700. The median for the group was 461. The estimated total number of full-time students in the 142 women's colleges combined was 6,900, approximately 24.5% of the estimated total in all Catholic colleges and universities for that year. The women's colleges accounted for approximately 55% of the Catholic institutions run primarily for the laity, but they enrolled only an estimated 26% of the full-time students in the lay institutions.

In addition to considerable differences among the women's colleges in size, the percentage increase or decrease in both first-time fall applications and full-time undergraduate enrollment from the year 1960-61 to 1964-65 differed considerably. In approximately 8% of the colleges reporting, the number of first-time applications had increased during the four-year period. In 10% of the institutions, the average annual increase was less than 3%. On the other hand, in approximately 40% of these colleges, the average annual increase was in excess of 12%. As for the decrease or increase in the full-time undergraduate enrollment, while the median cumulative four-year percentage increase for the colleges reporting was 30%, or some 7% annually, one-fourth of the institutions had realized a cumulative four-year increase of less than 12%, and another 25% had experienced a cumulative four-year increase in excess of 50%. Only 5% of the women's colleges reporting had fewer full-time undergraduate students in 1964-65 than they had four years earlier. However, approximately 40% had realized an average annual increase during that period of less than 3%.

Information with regard to the percentage of first-time applicants being admitted in the fall of 1964 showed a median of 60%. In 25% of the institutions, less than four out of ten were accepted, while in another 25% an average of more than seven out of ten were accepted.

Twenty-three of the 118 four-year Catholic colleges for women offered graduate programs in 1964-65. Without exception, the programs were limited to the master's level. Although 20% of the four-year colleges did offer graduate work, the number of full-time graduate students was quite small. Only 3% of the total full-time students enrolled in the Level III women's colleges were involved in full-time graduate work during the regular academic year. The vast majority of graduate education was done during the summer or on a part-time basis during regular sessions. A comparison of the quartile figures for full-time, part-time and summer graduate enrollments in the graduate women's colleges reporting for 1964-65 (Table 23) shows the big difference in medians. Over one-half of the colleges enrolled fewer than nine full-time graduate students. Six had no full-time graduate students at all, and only three had more than 50. The largest full-time graduate enrollment reported was 124. The figures for part-time graduate students are considerably higher, with a median of 88. Three institutions reported part-time graduate enrollments in excess of 200. There were approximately five times as many part-time as full-time graduate students reported. However, the most extensive graduate programs were carried on in the summer. The median for the institutions reporting was 256, with four institutions enrolling more than 400 graduate students during the summer of 1965. The total summer graduate enrollment for the women's colleges was approximately ten times the full-time graduate enrollment during the regular sessions.

Faculty

The estimated total number of full-time faculty, both religious and lay, in the 142 women's colleges in 1964-65 was 5,350, an estimated 24.5% of the total in all Catholic colleges and universities for that year. The women's colleges represented 31% of all the Catholic institutions of higher learning, enrolled 28.9% of the full-time students attending Catholic institutions, and engaged 24.5% of the full-time faculty. With regard to the number of full-time faculty in individual colleges for women, the median for those reporting was 34. In 25% of the institutions there were fewer than 25 full-time faculty members, and in another 25% more than 60. Compared with the men's colleges and the coed institutions, the women's colleges made less use of part-time faculty. For those reporting, the median percentage of the faculty which was part-time in 1964-65 was 31%. In only one-fourth of the institutions did this percentage exceed 40%; in one-fourth of the institutions it was less than 23%. With regard to the percentage of full-time lay faculty, the percentages for the women's colleges were considerably higher in general than was the case for any of the groups of institutions run primarily for religious or for the clergy. For the colleges reporting, the median percentage of the full-time faculty which was lay was 40%. In one-fourth of the institutions the percentage was lower than 27%, but in another one-fourth, over half of the full-time faculty was lay. As to the percentage of ranked faculty holding the doctorate, differences were again evident. The median percentage for the colleges reporting was 27%, but one-fourth of the institutions reported a percentage lower than 20%, and another one-fourth a percentage higher than 31%.

Current Income

As was the case for all of the class groups, the amount of total current income for each of the women's colleges was related to the size of the institution. The median for the group reporting was $721,000, with one-fourth realizing an annual current income in 1964-65 in excess of $1,000,000, and another one-fourth below $380,000. The estimated total current income in 1964-65 for the 142 women's colleges as a group was $120,000,000, approximately 26.4% of the estimated total for that year for all Catholic institutions. It may be noted that this figure is in line with that (24.5%) representing the percentage of full-time students in all Catholic institutions enrolled in the Catholic women's colleges.

For all the Catholic institutions run primarily for lay students, the principal source of current income was tuition and fees. For the women's colleges reporting, the median percentage of total current income coming from this source was 65%. In only 25% of the women's colleges reporting did tuition and fees constitute less than one-half of the total current income for 1964-65. In one-fourth of the institutions tuition and fees accounted for at least 80% of the total. Apart from tuition and fees, the only other substantial source of operational income for the women's colleges was that coming by way of gifts from other than religious sources. For the institutions reporting, the median percentage from such gifts was 7%. In

25% of the institutions more than 15% of the total current income for 1964-65 came from gifts from other than religious sources. As was true for the men's institutions, the percentage of current income which came from endowment, the federal government or gifts from religious sources was generally small. The median from endowment for the institutions reporting was only 1%, with only 25% of the institutions getting more than 2% of their total current income from endowment. Only one-fourth of the institutions reported more than 1% from federal sources. As for gifts from religious sources, the median percentage of total current income for the colleges reporting was 0%, with only one-fourth of the institutions reporting a figure as high as 8%.

Capital Funds

During the five-year period 1960-61 to 1964-65, the 142 women's colleges as a group raised an estimated total of $185,000,000 in capital funds. The median five-year figure for the colleges reporting was slightly over $1,000,000. Again, however, there was considerable diversity among institutions in amounts raised. In 25% of those colleges reporting, the total amount during the five-year period was less than $600,000, while in another one-fourth of the institutions the amount exceeded $2,000,000. The $185,000,000 total combined capital funds raised by the 142 women's colleges represented approximately 33% of the total raised by all Catholic colleges and universities for the five-year period. Recalling the fact that the women's colleges enrolled approximately 24.5% of the full-time students in all Catholic institutions for 1964-65, and received 26.4% of the total Catholic current income, a greater disproportion can be noted between the full-time student percentage and that for capital funds than was true for the student percentage and that for current income. The data suggest that arguments for greater consolidation among the women's colleges should be based on the capital fund drain rather than on charges that an excessive percentage of the operational income is going to these institutions.

As for the source of the capital funds raised by the women's colleges, surprisingly small amounts came by way of gifts from either the sponsoring religious order or the diocese, although there was a great difference among the institutions reporting. Over half of the women's colleges reporting received no capital funds from such religious sources. However, in 25% of the colleges more than 25% of the capital funds raised by each of these institutions did come from either the order or the diocese.

Problems

Finding sufficient financial resources is the most critical problem facing all Catholic colleges and universities. The need for money exists in all types of institutions, but the particular financial problems of the women's colleges differ somewhat from those of the larger institutions. More so than the latter, the colleges for women have depended more heavily in the recent past on members of the religious order for staffing the institutions. As a result, the total amount paid for faculty and administrative salaries was within reach of the typical sources of income. However, the gradual increase in the number of full-time, qualified lay faculty and the recent emphasis on getting laymen for some of the top administrative positions have significantly increased expenses, which the colleges are finding more and more difficult to meet without substantial increases in both the amount and sources of income. Many institutions are at the point where a further increase in tuition would hurt enrollments. Since the religious orders themselves cannot be expected to subsidize the institution to any substantially greater degree, the additional income has to come from gifts. The question of whether the women's colleges will be successful in raising enough funds to pick up operational deficits will be critical to their future.

Apart from the major question of financing, another related problem must be solved by the women's colleges—that of definition. In the past, the almost exclusive use of members of the controlling religious order to fill trusteeships and administrative positions in the college, as well as the heavy numerical dominance of religious on the faculties, effected a very close identification of the institution with the order. As the colleges move toward greater involvement of laymen at all levels, this identification is reduced. There are advantages, both fiscal and professional, in the loss of such identification, but there are also problems. Apart from the increase in expense already noted, there is the problem of maintaining a unique institutional image. Where there are two or three women's colleges in the same metropolitan area, the uniqueness has more frequently been based on the distinction between or among the controlling religious orders than on any demonstrated difference in goals or programs of the colleges themselves. As the latter become less identified with the controlling order, the difference between one Catholic women's college and another becomes harder to define. As a result, fund-raising in a competitive era becomes even more difficult. Discerning donors are becoming more reluctant to give money to what appears to be a duplication of effort. In addition to the continual battle that development officers in the women's colleges must wage in the day of coed institutions, the challenge to maintain uniqueness within these institutions themselves is indeed great.

A final problem typical of the women's college has developed from one of its traditional appeals—smallness and informality. Historically, the opportunities open to the student in a small college with a sort of "family spirit" have been one of the principal reasons why a Catholic girl has chosen one of the women's colleges. Part of this family spirit has been a flavor of informality. Although much of this has accrued to the institution's advantage, habits of informality have created problems. When the control and staffing of the institution were more closely tied to the religious order, lack of formal procedures caused little concern. However, as laymen become more heavily involved, this informality tended to be viewed as a lack of professionalism. The process of becoming more formal without loss of familiarity can be a delicate matter; it is certainly a matter of concern in many of the women's colleges.

Strengths

Attacking some of the very problems more typical of the women's colleges has resulted in the more typical strengths. Those institutions which have faced the challenge of finding additional support, of making decisions regarding control and identification with the parent order, and of providing something unique have been forced to a basic redefinition. This has led to a willingness to gamble on new experiments and emphases, to an attitude of openness to fundamental change which has created a spirit of optimism and enthusiasm. This must be recognized as one of the strengths of the women's colleges as a group.

Further, many of the colleges have met the problems created by informality and, with regard to the implementation of fiscal, academic and extracurricular procedures, have been more in line with policies more typical of larger institutions. This has been done in many cases without sacrifice of the spirit of informality, which continues to be one of the attractive features of the relatively small women's college.

Implications for Catholic Higher Education

There are several reasons why the current problems and strengths of the women's colleges should be recognized by other Catholic colleges and universities. For one thing, they represent some 142 institutions, and the future of these can have a considerable impact on the others. As the women's colleges review their goals and search for definition, the potential of new forms of cooperation and involvement with other institutions cannot be overlooked. If the larger institutions recognize the contribution that the women's college can make and if they are willing to approach the matter of cooperation on terms other than those set by themselves, a much more effective pattern of consolidation could be realized. As the women's colleges prepare for decisions with long-range implications, the attitude toward cooperation and involvement they find in other Catholic institutions will be a significant factor as to whether real consolidation of Catholic effort will materialize.

Renewal and redefinition are becoming typical of women's colleges. If all Catholic institutions were as willing to consider fundamental reassessment of goals, policies, and procedures as are many in the women's group, the future of Catholic higher education could be exciting indeed.

Coeducational Institutions

One purpose of the extensive numerical and percentage breakdowns for Catholic institutions of higher learning presented in

Chapter I was to caution the reader against unwarranted generalizations about the form and structure of Catholic higher education. That same word of caution is reiterated with regard to the coeducational institutions, since there is a tendency to think of this group as the large Catholic universities. It is a fact that coeducational institutions accounted for over one-half of the 29 Catholic institutions with full-time enrollments in excess of 2,000, but only 25% of the coeducational institutions themselves were that large. The specific numerical breakdown for the coeducational institutions for 1964-65 by level and size is presented in Table 24.

TABLE 24

Distribution of Coeducational Institutions
By Level and Size, 1964-65

	Full-Time Enrollment					
	0 - 100	101 - 300	301 - 750	751 - 2000	2000+	Total
Level I	2	4	2	—	—	8
Level II	1	3	16	9	—	29
Level III	—	—	2	6	8	16
Level IV	—	—	—	2	8	10
Total	3	7	20	17	16	63

Table 24 shows that 26 of the coeducational institutions (41%) awarded at least the master's degree in 1964-65 and that slightly less than one-half had fewer than 750 full-time students. There were 16 coeducational institutions at the bachelor's level which had between 301 and 750 full-time students. To the figures in Table 24 may be added the fact that 55 of the 63 coeducational institutions were regionally accredited and 53 were opened before 1950.

As was the case for men's institutions and the women's colleges, most of the coeducational Catholic colleges and universities were under the control of either a religious order or a diocese. Again, there was the current trend toward greater involvement of laymen on the governing boards of the institutions. For the coeducational institutions reporting, the size of the governing boards varied considerably, with some having as many as 19 members and others only 3. The median size for those institutions reporting was 7. In

1964-65, 13 of the 50 coeducational institutions reporting had laymen on the governing board. In one institution only, however, did they constitute a majority. This trend seems to be gaining momentum and the future should see more and more Catholic colleges and universities moving in the direction of boards on which laymen predominate. In 1964-65, however, laymen were involved in the governance of the Catholic institutions most frequently through membership on advisory boards of trustees. For the coeducational institutions reporting, all but 3 had advisory boards, ranging in size from as many as 55 to as few as 5, with a median of 26. Laymen dominated numerically on all of these boards. Campus interviews revealed that as institutions moved to greater involvement of laymen on governing boards, the advisory boards were either been discontinued or assigned a more limited function, usually that of public relations.

Table 25 presents quartile points for a number of statistical dimensions for the 50 coeducational institutions which completed the survey form distributed by the research staff. The data provide information both with regard to the point about which these institutions tend to cluster and the degree of diversity within the group. This information is discussed briefly in the paragraphs below.

Enrollment

The median full-time enrollment for the coeducational colleges and universities reporting was 800. Approximately one-fourth of the institutions reported enrollments of less than 200, with another 25% having more than 2,000. The estimated total full-time enrollment for the 63 coeducational institutions combined for 1964-65 was 109,000, approximately 38.5% of the estimated total in all Catholic colleges and universities for that year. Hence, while coeducational institutions represented only 13.8% of all Catholic colleges and universities, they educated almost 40% of the full-time students. Data for the relative increase or decrease in both first-time applications and full-time undergraduate enrollments for the year 1964-65 over 1960-61 show that some of the coeducational institutions grew con-

TABLE 25

COEDUCATIONAL INSTITUTIONS

ENROLLMENT, FACULTY, FUNDS—QUARTILE POINTS

	IQ	Median	3Q
Enrollment			
Full-Time Total, 1964-65	437	800	2165
% Increase Full-Time Undergrad., 1961-65	14%	40%	54%
Full-Time Graduate, 1964-65	45	200	477
Part-Time Graduate, 1964-65	233	625	1220
Summer Graduate, 1965	162	565	1200
Faculty			
Full-Time Total, 1964-65	35	70	123
% Faculty Part-Time, 1964-65	17%	33%	43%
% Full-Time Faculty Lay, 1964-65	50%	73%	78%
% Ranked Faculty with Doctorate, 1964-65	21%	30%	43%
Funds			
Total Current Income, 1964-65 (Thousands)	558	1129	3126
% Tuition and fees	52%	69%	86%
% Endowment	0%	1%	3%
% Federal Government	0%	0%	5%
% Gifts from religious sources	0%	0%	2%
% Gifts, *not* religious sources	2%	9%	20%
Total Capital Funds, 1960-65 (Thousands)	604	1826	3691
% Gifts from Religious Sources	0%	1%	25%

siderably while others did not. Fourteen percent of the institutions reporting had fewer first-time applications in 1964-65 than they had four years earlier. In 22% of the institutions reporting, the cumulative percent increase was less than 15%, or an annual average of less than 4%. On the other hand, in one-third of the institutions the average annual increase was better than 15%. With regard to the increase or decrease over the four-year period in full-time undergraduate enrollment, the same individual differences can be noted. The median cumulative four-year percentage increase for the institutions reporting was 40%, an average of 10% per year. In 25% of the institutions, however, the average annual increase was no better than 3%. Eleven percent reported fewer full-time undergraduates in 1964-65 than in 1960-61. On the other hand, approximately 25% of the institutions had realized a cumulative percentage increase of greater than 54%, or an annual average greater than 9%.

The coeducational institutions carried on most of the full-time graduate work in Catholic higher education. It is estimated that slightly over 70% of all the full-time graduate students in Catholic colleges and universities in 1964-65 were in coeducational institutions. The men's colleges enrolled approximately 25%, with some 4% in women's colleges. As was the case with both the men's and women's institutions, full-time graduate work was not as extensive in the coeducational institutions as part-time and summer programs were. The median full-time graduate enrollment for the institutions reporting was 200, with 25% of the institutions enrolling fewer than 45 and another 25% enrolling more than 500. The part-time median was 625, with only 25% of the institutions enrolling fewer than 200 and another 25% enrolling more than 1,200. As for summer graduate enrollments, the median for the institutions reporting was 565, with 25% having fewer than 162 summer graduate students and 25% enrolling more than 1,200. As was true for the men's colleges, the number of graduates in summer and part-time programs during the regular academic year was about the same. In the women's colleges, the summer graduate programs were much larger than either the part-time or the full-time programs during the regular sessions.

Figures showing the percentage of the first-time applicants which were being admitted in 1964-65 indicate a median of 65%, or slightly more than six of every ten students. At one end of the scale, 25% of the institutions were admitting less than four out of every ten first-time applicants, while 25% of the institutions were admitting more than eight out of every ten.

Faculty

There were more full-time students and more full-time faculty members in Catholic coeducational institutions than there were in any of the other classes in 1964-65. With regard to the full-time faculty, the estimated total teaching in the 63 institutions was 6,700, approximately 36.3% of the full-time faculty in all Catholic colleges and universities for that year. Although the coeducational institutions represented only 13.8% of all the Catholic colleges and universities, they enrolled 38.8% of all the full-time students and engaged 36.3% of all the full-time faculty in Catholic institutions. Paralleling the difference in size among the coeducational institutions were differences in the size of full-time faculties. For the institutions reporting, the median full-time faculty was 70. Twenty-five percent of the institutions had fewer than 35 full-time faculty members, but another group representing 25% had full-time faculties larger than 125.

Differences were also evident among the institutions as to the percentage of the total faculty which was part-time. The median percentage for the institutions reporting was 33%, but in 25% of the institutions less than 17% of the total faculty was part-time, and in another 25% of the institutions the part-time faculty represented more than 43% of the total.

With regard to the percentage of laymen on the full-time faculty, the data indicate more extensive use of laymen in the coeducational institutions than was the case for any of the other five classes of Catholic institutions. The median percentage of full-time faculty which was lay for the coeducational institutions reporting was 73%. In only one-fourth of the coeducational institutions did the full-time religious faculty outnumber the full-time lay faculty. In 25% of the coeducational institutions, the percentage of laymen on the faculty exceeded 78%.

Considerable differences were evident with regard to the percentage of the ranked faculty holding the doctorate in the coeducational institutions. The median for those reporting was 30%, with one-fourth of the institutions reporting less than 21%, and another 25% of the institutions reporting a percentage greater than 43%.

Current Income

As was the case for full-time students and full-time faculty, the amount of current income realized in 1964-65 by the group of 63 coeducational institutions was larger than that for any of the other five categories. The median total current income figure for the institutions reporting was $1,129,000. Again, diversity is evident from the fact that while 25% of the institutions reporting realized a total current income for that year of less than $550,000, another one-fourth of the institutions had total current incomes in excess of $3,100,000. The estimated total current income for the coeducational institutions as a group in 1964-65 was $156,000,000, approximately 34.4% of the estimated total for all Catholic colleges and universities for that year. This percentage of 34.4% was slightly less than the 38.8% of full-time students in the coeducational institutions and the 36.3% of the full-time faculty. Again, although there were some differences among coeducational institutions as to specific percentages, the largest single source of current income was tuition and fees, as was true for both the men's and women's institutions run for laymen. The median percentage of the total current income which came from tuition and fees for the coeducational institutions reporting was 69%. However, in 25% of the institutions, tuition and fees accounted for less than 50% of the total current income, and in another 25% tuition and fees made up more than 86% of the total current income for 1964-65.

Although less significant than tuition and fees, the second principal source of operational income was gifts from other than religious sources. The median for the coeducational institutions reporting was 9%. Twenty-five percent of the institutions got less than 2% of their total current income from gifts other than religious sources, while in another 25% of the institutions such gifts accounted for more than 20% of the total.

As was true for the other five class categories income from endowment, the federal government, and gifts from religious sources was relatively insignificant. With regard to endowment income, the median percentage of total current income coming from this source for the coeducational institutions reporting was a mere 1%. In fact, in only 25% of the coeducational institutions reporting did the endowment income account for more than 3% of the total current income for that year. As to funds from the federal government, over one-half of the institutions reporting received no federal funds at all for the operations. On the other hand, 25% of the coeducational institutions (generally the larger institutions) reported that more than 5% of their total current income for 1964-65 came from the federal government in the form of research or training grants. As to gifts from either the sponsoring religious order or the diocese, the median percentage of total current income for the coeducational institutions reporting was again 0%. In fact, in only 25% of the institutions reporting did gifts from religious sources constitute more than 2% of the total current income for 1964-65.

Capital Funds

Differences were evident among the coeducational institutions in the total amounts of capital funds raised in the five-year period immediately preceding 1964-65. The total amount of capital funds raised by the coeducational colleges as a group was larger than that for any of the other five categories. It was estimated for the five year period at $160,000,000, approximately 28.7% of the estimated total for all Catholic colleges and universities for that year. The percentage is somewhat lower than the 38.8% for full-time students. It might be recalled that for the institutions run primarily for religious the percentage of total capital funds realized by these institutions was larger than the percentage of full-time students being educated. Although the estimated total amount of capital funds raised by the coeducational institutions was larger than it was for any of the other five categories, the percentage of such funds going to the coeducational institutions was less than the percentage of full-time students being educated. The differences were considerable among the coeducational institutions with regard to the amount of capital funds raised. The median for the five-year period immediately preceding 1964-65 was $1,826,000. However, 25% of the institutions raised a five-year total of less than $600,000, and another group representing 25% raised more than $3,600,000 each during that five-year period. As to the percentage of capital funds which came from either the sponsoring religious order or the diocese, the median for the institutions reporting was a mere 1%. In fact, in only 25% of the coeducational institutions reporting did gifts from religious sources represent more than 25% of the total amount of capital funds raised.

The Larger Institutions

The data presented and discussed above were reported by Catholic coeducational institutions at all levels and of all sizes. Campus interviews revealed that the problems and strengths of the smaller coeducational institutions did not differ substantially from some of those of either the smaller religious institutions or the smaller men's or women's colleges, but that the large institutions did have unique characteristics as a group. The brief summary of problems, strengths and implications which follows is limited to those of the larger coeducational institutions and would also be typical of the very large universities run primarily for men.

Problems

The most critical problem for the larger Catholic institutions, particularly the more complex universities, is that of finding adequate financial support. As these institutions struggle to remain competitive at the graduate and professional levels, and as the cost of this phase of higher education continues to escalate enormously, their dependence on sources of income other than tuition increases annually. Although they are receiving increasing amounts of federal funds and monies from private foundations, Catholic institutions need more income from unrestricted gifts to meet operational expenses. Many Catholic administrators in the larger universities are convinced that, unless new sources of operational funds become available, the institutions will have to settle for programs less ambitious and below the academic potential anticipated if financial support were available. Administrators seem convinced that the failure of Catholic universities to reach the "top 50" is due primarily to the lack of sufficient financial resources, not either to lack of academic potential or to supposed restrictions on academic freedom or to institutional autonomy.

Added to the difficulty of securing development income for operations is that of keeping enrollments up to sufficient levels. Increasing tuition rates, combined with the growing number of urban junior colleges and extensions of state universities, are reducing the pool of local students available to Catholic institutions. As a result, many of the large urban Catholic universities are becoming much more quickly and heavily residential than was anticipated.

Another disturbing problem for the large institution is that of finding program designs which will implement the institution's commitment to the importance and value of each and every student. How to provide adequate attention to individual student talent and needs is a critical problem for all large universities. However, for Catholic institutions the commitment to development of religious and spiritual values makes the problem more difficult and complex. Interviewees frequently complained that the effect of the larger Catholic universities on the religious attitudes of the students on the whole was minimal. Finding contemporary solutions to this perennial problem represents an immense challenge to the larger Catholic institutions.

Closely related to the problem of effectively influencing student values and attitudes is the basic difficulty of defining a Catholic university. These institutions have necessarily imitated their secular counterparts to remain competitive. To avoid loss of special identity in the process has been extremely difficult.

A final weakness brought out frequently by interviewees, and one usually traced to rapid expansion, is the failure of the large institutions to develop policies and management talent and efficiency comparable to growth in size and complexity. Understandably, institutions already spread thin have chosen to put priority on critical faculty and facility needs rather than seeing to adequate administrative staff support. As a result, some of the institutions have outgrown their management.

Strengths

Because the larger institutions educate a heavy proportion of the students in Catholic colleges and universities and engage a similar proportion of faculty, their achievements are primarily responsible for whatever prestige is enjoyed by Catholic higher education. The stronger academic departments are typically found in the larger Catholic institutions, as well as a pool of administrators who have earned both the recognition and respect of American higher education. The record of many of the larger Catholic institutions in terms of the production of professional talent also figures as a strength. In addition, a good percentage of undergraduates from these larger institutions go on to graduate and professional work in outstanding non-Catholic universities.

Interviewees stressed still another strength typical of the larger Catholic institution—that of significant service to the civic community. Most of these Catholic institutions are urban and are heavily involved in community activities, a contribution which many of the state universities are only now beginning to match as urban branches become better established.

Finally, the larger Catholic institutions seem to be taking a greater interest in helping smaller institutions find more adequate arrangements for enhancing their academic potential. With the growing recognition that the larger institutions may have something to gain from the smaller college, cooperative efforts are developing rapidly. Further, examples set by the larger institutions in terms of control and management restructuring are serving as models for many of the smaller institutions.

Implications for Catholic Higher Education

Since the larger institutions are, for better or for worse, the showplace of Catholic higher education, what happens to these institutions will have a far-reaching effect on all Catholic institutions. Already the publicity given unfortunate episodes of faculty trouble in one or two large institutions has put all of Catholic higher education under suspicion. Similarly, the move of several large institutions toward greater involvement of laymen on governing boards has created a climate of national attention.

However, the most fundamental reason why all Catholic colleges must be concerned with and interested in the larger Catholic institutions is that if the latter cannot successfully press the argument for adequate financial support, the future of Catholic higher education will not be bright. Whether the position is justified or not, the attitude of private business, the academic world and the American public toward the larger Catholic institutions will determine to a great extent the future of all Catholic institutions of higher learning. It would appear that the smaller institutions should put aside their competition with and fear of the larger institutions and work with them to insure that all available resources are used intelligently. This is not to suggest the demise of smaller institutions but simply to encourage the discontinuation of splintered, uncoordinated, or debilitating efforts. There seems to be no question but that the attitude of the smaller institution toward the larger should be one of genuine cooperation rather than of fearful isolation. Unless the stronger survive—and survive with excellence—there is little hope for the weaker.

CHAPTER FIVE

Comparison by Class, Size and Level

Throughout the preceding chapter, the statistical information was organized and presented for each of the six class categories of Catholic colleges and universities. There was occasional comparison between classes, but it was not extensive. Emphasis was on the considerable diversity within each of the class groups, a diversity which would have been evidenced had categories of either size or level been used instead of class. The present chapter has been organized in such a way as to highlight differences not within a given class, size or level category, but between or among the subcategories of each. It has to be recognized that while a given women's college may in structure and operation more closely parallel a given men's college than it does other women's colleges, there are differences between the men's colleges *as a group* and the women's colleges, between the smallest institutions and the largest, and between the junior colleges and the doctoral institutions.

Tables 26 through 29 compare the different class, size and level categories in terms of the percentage of Catholic institutions represented by each of the subcategories, the percentage of the estimated total full-time enrollment in Catholic institutions, the percentage of full-time faculty, of total current income, and of total capital funds raised from 1960 to 1965. Tables 30 through 41 present comparisons of categories and subcategories in terms of median figures relating to enrollment, faculty and finances. The percentages in Tables 26 through 29 are based on the following figures:

Number of Catholic colleges and universities, 1964-65—	457
Estimated total full-time enrollment, 1964-65 —	281,000
Estimated total full-time faculty, 1964-65 —	18,500
Estimated total current income, 1964-65 —	$455,000,000
Estimated total capital funds raised from 1960 to 1965—	$560,000,000

TABLE 26

COMPARISON OF RELIGIOUS VS. LAY BY
PERCENTAGE OF TOTAL INSTITUTIONS, STUDENTS, FACULTY, FUNDS

1964-65	Inst. For Religious	Inst. For Laity
% Total Catholic Institutions	43.8%	56.2%
% Total Full-Time Students	7.3%	92.7%
% Total Full-Time Faculty	9.4%	90.6%
% Total Current Income	8.0%	92.0%
% Capital Funds (1960-65)	18.6%	81.4%

HIGHLIGHTS–TABLE 26

1. The institutions for religious (72 religious seminaries, 74 Sister formation colleges, 54 diocesan seminaries) represented 43.8% of the Catholic colleges and universities, but enrolled only 7.3% of the estimated total full-time students in all of the Catholic institutions.

2. The relative percentages for the two groups of institutions were consistent for full-time students, full-time faculty, and current income. However, the institutions run for lay students got "less than their share" of capital funds.

TABLE 27

COMPARISON OF CLASS GROUPS BY
PERCENTAGE OF TOTAL INSTITUTIONS, STUDENTS, FACULTY, FUNDS

	RM	RW	DC	LM	LW	C
% Total Catholic Institutions	15.8%	16.2%	11.8%	11.4%	31.0%	13.8%
% Total Full-Time Students	1.8%	1.2%	4.3%	29.4%	24.5%	38.8%
% Total Full-Time Faculty	3.2%	1.9%	4.3%	25.4%	28.9%	36.3%
% Total Current Income	2.6%	1.1%	4.3%	31.2%	26.4%	34.4%
% Total Capital Funds	7.1%	4.4%	7.1%	19.7%	33.0%	28.7%

HIGHLIGHTS–TABLE 27

1. The 52 men's colleges (lay) educated more full-time students than the 142 women's colleges.

2. The greatest disproportion between the percentage of institutions represented and the percentage of full-time students enrolled occurred in the Sister formation college group (16.2% vs. 1.2%).

3. For the institutions run for the laity, in only the coeducational institutions as a group was the percentage of estimated total current income less than the percentage of estimated total full-time students.

4. For the institutions run for the laity, in only the women's colleges did the percentage of estimated total capital funds raised exceed the percentage of estimated total full-time students.

TABLE 28

COMPARISON OF SIZE GROUPS BY
PERCENTAGE OF TOTAL INSTITUTIONS, STUDENTS, FACULTY, FUNDS

	Full-Time Enrollment				
	0 - 100	101 - 300	301 - 750	751 - 2000	2000+
% Total Catholic Institutions	36.1%	19.3%	23.0%	15.3%	6.3%
% Total Full-Time Students	2.8%	6.7%	19.2%	27.2%	44.1%
% Total Full-Time Faculty	5.4%	7.6%	21.6%	28.1%	37.3%
% Total Current Income	3.5%	6.8%	16.5%	28.1%	45.1%
% Total Capital Funds	17.8%	13.9%	22.3%	26.3%	19.7%

HIGHLIGHTS—TABLE 28

1. The two largest size groups combined represented only 21.6% of the institutions, but educated 71.3% of the estimated total full-time students in all Catholic colleges and universities.

2. The greatest disproportion between the percentage of institutions and the percentage of estimated total full-time students occurred in the smallest and the largest size groups.

3. The largest size group was the only one in which the percentage of estimated total full-time students exceeded the percentage of estimated total full-time faculty.

4. Only in the institutions enrolling between 351 and 750 full-time students was the percentage of current income less than than that for full-time students enrolled.

5. The greatest disproportion between the percentage of estimated total full-time students enrolled and the percentage of estimated total capital funds raised occurred in the smallest and the largest size groups. The smallest size group enrolled only 2.8% of the full-time students in Catholic institutions but raised 17.8% of

the capital funds raised during the five-year period by all Catholic colleges and universities.

TABLE 29

COMPARISON OF LEVEL GROUPS BY
PERCENTAGE OF TOTAL INSTITUTIONS, STUDENTS, FACULTY, FUNDS

	Level I	Level II	Level III	Level IV
% Total Catholic Institutions	28.7%	50.3%	17.1%	3.9%
% Total Full-Time Students	3.8%	40.2%	29.8%	26.2%
% Total Full-Time Faculty	3.4%	37.3%	32.0%	27.3%
% Total Current Income	3.1%	36.0%	34.7%	26.3%
% Total Capital Funds	6.1%	50.1%	28.9%	14.9%

HIGHLIGHTS—TABLE 29

1. The percentage of institutions and the percentage of estimated total full-time students enrolled were almost reversed for the Level I and Level IV groups.
2. More than was the case for the class or size breakdowns, there was greater consistency at all levels with regard to the percentages of estimated total full-time students and the percentage of estimated total current income.
3. The Level I and II groups got "more than their share" of capital funds; the Level IV institutions got considerably "less than their share."

TABLE 30

FULL-TIME UNDERGRADUATES 1964-65
BY CLASS, SIZE, LEVEL GROUPS

Median			Class			
	RM	RW	DC	LM	LW	C
	66	37	119	1116	455	800
Full-Time Under-Grad.			Size (Full-Time Enrollment)			
	0-100	101-300	301-750	751-2000	2000+	
	43	192	483	934	3000	
			Level			
	I	II	III	IV		
	62	418	875	3800		

HIGHLIGHTS—TABLE 30

1. The median full-time enrollment for the Sister formation colleges was only 37.
2. The largest median on a basis of class was the men's institutions (lay).
3. The median for the Level I institutions (largely religious) was only 62.

TABLE 31

CUMULATIVE % INCREASE, FULL-TIME UNDERGRADS 1961-65
BY CLASS, SIZE, LEVEL GROUPS

Median	RM	RW	Class DC	LM	LW	C
	12%	5%	3%	18%	30%	40%
Cumulative			**Size** (Full-Time Enrollment)			
4-year	0-100	101-300	301-750	751-2000	2000+	
Increase	4%	22%	22%	19%	29%	
			Level			
	I	II	III	IV		
	11%	22%	17%	24%		

HIGHLIGHTS—TABLE 31

1. In general, there was a smaller median percentage increase for the institutions run for religious or the clergy than for the institutions run primarily for the laity.
2. The greatest median increase was in the coeducational institutions.
3. There was a smaller median increase for the men's colleges than for the women's.
4. There was a considerably larger median percentage increase for the largest size institutions than for the smallest. The medians for the middle size groups were approximately the same.
5. The median percentage increase was higher for the bachelor and doctoral level institutions than for the junior colleges and the master's level institutions.

6. Combining the figures for class, size and level, the smallest median percentage increases were in small junior colleges run for religious; the largest were in large doctoral level coeducational institutions.

TABLE 32

% FACULTY PART-TIME, 1964-65
BY CLASS, SIZE, LEVEL GROUPS

Median			Class			
	RM	RW	DC	LM	LW	C
	22%	69%	39%	24%	31%	33%
% Part-Time Faculty			Size (Full-Time Enrollment)			
	0-100	101-300	301-750	751-2000	2000+	
	53%	38%	31%	21%	31%	
			Level			
	I	II	III	IV		
	61%	30%	26%	25%		

HIGHLIGHTS—TABLE 32

1. For the institutions run primarily for the laity, the median percentages of part-time faculty were similar for each of the groups.

2. A large difference in percentage of part-time faculty was evidenced by the medians for the religious seminaries (22%), and the Sister formation colleges (69%).
(N.B. Although no specific data was requested on this point, interviews suggested that this difference was at least partially due to the fact that the religious seminaries concentrate heavily on two fields (theology and philosophy), while the Sister formation colleges attempt to offer broader liberal arts programs and rely heavily on part-time teaching.)

3. In over one-half of the institutions with fewer than 100 full-time students, at least half of the faculty was part-time.

4. The lowest median percentage part-time faculty of all groups was reported by the institutions with full-time enrollments of between 351 and 750, even though this same size group had relatively fewer full-time faculty members than full-time students relative to the rest of the size groupings (see Table 28).

5. The median percentage of part-time faculty for Level I institutions was considerably higher than that for the other three levels.

TABLE 33

% Lay (Full-Time) Faculty, 1964-65
By Class, Size, Level Groups

Median			Class			
	RM	RW	DC	LM	LW	C
	0%	0%	0%	69%	40%	73%
			Size (Full-Time Enrollment)			
%	0-100	101-300	301-750	751-2000	2000+	
Lay	0%	19%	44%	61%	77%	
			Level			
	I	II	III	IV		
	0%	38%	55%	79%		

HIGHLIGHTS—TABLE 33

1. With regard to class, three facts emerged: very little use of full-time laymen in institutions run for the religious or the clergy; considerable use of laymen in the women's colleges; heavy involvement on the part of full-time lay faculty in the men's colleges and coeducational institutions.

2. The median of 0% for the smallest institutions and the Level I institutions was due primarily to the fact that the greater proportion of these two groups consisted of institutions run for religious or for the clergy.

TABLE 34

% (Ranked Faculty) With Doctorate, 1964-65
By Class, Size, Level Groups

Median			Class			
	RM	RW	DC	LM	LW	C
	30%	23%	43%	35%	27%	30%
			Size (Full-Time Enrollment)			
%	0-100	101-300	301-750	751-2000	2000+	
Doctorate	22%	28%	27%	31%	43%	
			Level			
	I	II	III	IV		
	32%	69%	67%	60%		

HIGHLIGHTS—TABLE 34

1. The comparatively high median percentage for the diocesan seminaries is due to the number of faculty in these institutions holding the S.T.D. degree.

2. In general, the larger the institution and the higher its level, the greater the percentage of ranked faculty holding the doctor's degree.

TABLE 35

% Current Income From Tuition and Fees, 1964-65
By Class, Size, Level Groups

Median			Class			
	RM	RW	DC	LM	LW	C
	8%	15%	33%	80%	65%	69%
			Size (Full-Time Enrollment)			
	0-100	101-300	301-750	751-2000	2000+	
% From Tuition and Fees	19%	55%	71%	73%	72%	
			Level			
	I	II	III	IV		
	32%	69%	67%	60%		

HIGHLIGHTS—TABLE 35

1. The institutions for religious did not rely heavily on tuition income. The diocesan seminaries did so to a greater extent, but not by any means to the extent true for the institutions run for lay students.

2. The median percentage for current income represented by tuition and fees for the men's institutions was higher than that for both the women's colleges and the coeducational institutions.

3. The principal explanation for the lower medians for the two smallest size groups and the Level I group was the fact that a high percentage of the institutions in these three groups were run for religious.

4. The size of the institution as such makes relatively little difference on the whole with regard to the percentage of current income coming from tuition and fees.

5. The median for the doctoral level institutions was lower than that for the bachelor level or master's, partly because of the heavier proportion of the Federal research funds. (See Table 37.)
6. The institution most likely to rely heavily on tuition and fees would be the bachelor level men's college with between 751 and 2,000 full-time students.

TABLE 36

% Current Income From Endowment, 1964-65
By Class, Size, Level Groups

Median	RM	RW	Class DC	LM	LW	C
	0%	0%	2%	1%	1%	1%
			Size (Full-Time Enrollment)			
%	0-100	101-300	301-750	751-2000	2000+	
From Endow.	0%	0%	1%	1%	1%	
			Level			
	I	II	III	IV		
	0%	1%	1%	1%		

HIGHLIGHTS—TABLE 36

1. In general, Catholic colleges and universities recieved little of their annual current income from endowment. There were no general differences of class, level, or size in this regard.

TABLE 37

% Current Income From Federal Govt., 1964-65
By Class, Size, Level Groups

Median	RM	RW	Class DC	LM	LW	C
	0%	0%	0%	0%	0%	0%
			Size (Full-Time Enrollment)			
%	0-100	101-300	301-750	751-2000	2000+	
From Fed. Govt.	0%	0%	0%	0%	4%	
			Level			
	I	II	III	IV		
	0%	0%	1%	7%		

HIGHLIGHTS—TABLE 37

1. In general, the amount of federal funds received by the Catholic colleges and universities in terms of total current income was minimal.

2. The only group which differed consisted of the largest institution at the doctoral level, in which research funded by the federal government was considerable.

TABLE 38

% CURRENT INCOME FROM GIFTS FROM RELIGIOUS SOURCES
BY CLASS, SIZE, LEVEL GROUPS

Median			Class			
	RM	RW	DC	LM	LW	C
	54%	21%	12%	0%	0%	0%
			Size (Full-Time Enrollment)			
% From Gifts—Religious Sources	0-100	101-300	301-750	751-2000	2000+	
	45%	1%	0%	0%	0%	
			Level			
	I	II	III	IV		
	12%	1%	0%	0%		

HIGHLIGHTS—TABLE 38

1. Gifts from religious sources (usually subsidies from the controlling religious order) represented important sources of current income for the institutions run for religious but were negligible for those run for lay students. The high medians for the smallest size group and the Level I institutions were due again to the high proportion in these groups of institutions run for religious.

TABLE 39

% Current Income From Gifts, *Not* Religious Sources
By Class, Size, Level Groups

Median	RM	RW	Class DC	LM	LW	C
	7%	5%	10%	3%	7%	9%
			Size (Full-Time Enrollment)			
% Gifts, *Not* Religious Sources	0-100	101-300	301-750	751-2000	2000+	
	6%	8%	6%	4%	5%	
			Level			
	I	II	III	IV		
	4%	6%	3%	9%		

HIGHLIGHTS—TABLE 39

1. There was no great difference in general between institutions for religious or the diocesan clergy and the institutions run for lay students as to the percentage of current income coming from gifts other than from religious sources.
2. Again, no large differences in this variable were evident on a basis of class, size, or level.

TABLE 40

Capital Funds Raised—1960-1965
(Thousands)
By Class, Size, Level Groups

Median	RM	RW	Class DC	LM	LW	C
	624	210	590	1275	1016	1826
			Size (Full-Time Enrollment)			
Capital Funds Raised	0-100	101-300	301-750	751-2000	2000+	
	449	750	1013	1652	2847	
			Level			
	I	II	III	IV		
	259	1005	1900	3500		

HIGHLIGHTS—TABLE 40

1. The Sister formation colleges as a group raised fewer capital funds than did either the religious or diocesan seminaries.
2. Although the median size of the women's colleges was smaller, (less than half of the men's colleges), there was little difference in the median amount of the capital funds raised for the two groups.
3. The size of the institution, more than class or level, affected the amount of capital funds raised.

TABLE 41

% CAPITAL FUNDS FROM RELIGIOUS SOURCES BY CLASS, SIZE, LEVEL GROUPS

Median			Class			
	RM	RW	DC	LM	LW	C
	100%	64%	83%	0%	0%	1%
			Size (Full-Time Enrollment)			
%	0-100	101-300	301-750	751-2000	2000+	
Capital Funds From Religious Sources	100%	40%	0%	0%	0%	
			Level			
	I	II	III	IV		
	64%	1%	0%	0%		

HIGHLIGHTS—TABLE 41

1. The institutions run primarily for religious or the diocesan clergy received the greater portion of their capital funds from religious orders or the diocese. This was not the case for the institutions run for lay students.
2. The high medians for the two smaller size groups and the Level I institutions were due to the heavy proportion in these groups of institutions run for religious or for the diocesan clergy.